SOCIAL SPACES FOR OLDER QUEER ADULTS

Dr David Betts

SOCIAL SPACES FOR OLDER QUEER ADULTS

A Guide for Social Work Educators, Students, and Practitioners

The Queer and LGBT+ Studies Collection

Collection Editor
Seuta'afili Dr Patrick Thomsen

ᴌᴾᴾ

First published in 2023 by Lived Places Publishing

British Library Cataloguing in Publication Data
A CIP record for this book is available from the British Library

ISBN: 9781915734051 (pbk)
ISBN: 9781915734075 (ePDF)
ISBN: 9781915734068 (ePUB)

Cover design by Fiachra McCarthy
Book design by Rachel Trolove of Twin Trail Design
Typeset by Newgen Publishing UK

Lived Places Publishing
Long Island
New York 11789

www.livedplacespublishing.com

Abstract

This book explores how older queer adults navigate space, community, and social environments, and provides social workers with tools to support their wellbeing. It examines historical and contemporary experiences in Aotearoa New Zealand (Aotearoa is the contemporary Māori name for New Zealand), including political and legislative developments impacting older queer adults' wellbeing and sense of community. Highlighting the concept of the "queer unwanted," where many older queer adults are excluded from social environments due to their identity, the book also delves into queer ageing, addressing the specific concerns and needs of older members of the queer community. The book aims to provide insight for social work professionals, students, and educators to adapt their practice and support older queer adults.

Keywords

Community; wellbeing; policy; legislation; care services; sexual and gender diversity; queer unwanted; identity; lived experience

Acknowledgements

I am incredibly grateful to everyone who has assisted me and provided their support through the course of writing this book.

The most important people to mention are the participants who shared their stories and experiences with me. I wish to thank you all for the openness you showed me when you let me into your homes, your lives, and your communities. This book would not have been possible without the honest, transparent, and on occasion painful memories you shared with me. I value the time you contributed, and have learnt so much more from those experiences than I am able to present in this book alone.

I also wish to thank my family and friends for their support, in particular Annika for her constant friendship. I would not have been able to finish this book without you all.

Contents

Content warning

This book contains explicit references to, and descriptions of, experiences and situations which may cause distress. This includes references to and descriptions of:

- Social and cultural stigma towards the queer community, including homophobia and transphobia.
- Experiences of discrimination, prejudice, and abuse.
- Encounters with inappropriate and inadequate professional services, such as from doctors, psychiatrists, and social services.
- The resulting negative impact of these experiences on the mental health and wellbeing of older queer adults.

Please be aware that references to these potentially distressing topics occur *frequently* and *throughout* the book, and readers should prioritise their own mental health and wellbeing when reading this content.

1
Social spaces and older queer adults

Learning objective: to develop an understanding of the purpose and goals of the book

By reading this chapter, readers will be able to articulate the overall purpose and goals of the book, including identifying who would benefit from reading it or using it as an educational resource. Readers will gain insight into the significance of exploring how older queer adults navigate spaces and the impact on their wellbeing.

Learning objective: to become familiar with the terminology and research foundation

After studying this chapter, readers will be able to understand the language and terminology consistently used throughout the book, and understand the rationale behind its selection. They will also gain knowledge about the research sources and research foundations that the book draws upon.

Introduction

> Twenty years ago there was no narrative. There was not even references to other people like myself. It was a profoundly life-changing event to meet other people like myself and to end that extreme isolation that I felt. And I think what I would say about that – and I'd say it to you as a social worker and myself as a therapist – we know that community, a sense of belonging, is so paramount to good health. I don't think we talk about this enough. For quite a long period of doing this work, most of the people that I work with saw themselves within the binary way of looking at things. To step outside that social construction both required a headspace, a willingness to do that, and an immense amount of bravery.
>
> (Rowan,[1] 62)

The central question I was interested in while writing this book was "how do older queer adults navigate space, community, and social environments?" This question contains multiple broad and encompassing concepts. From the notion of space and spatial relationships, community development and inclusion, to the structural forces shaping social environments – this book aims to explore how older queer adults engage with the world around them. More than that, the goal of this book is to do so in such a manner that is beneficial for social workers – for students, practitioners, and educators – who work alongside and with older queer adults. Drawing from a PhD research project with older queer adults from Aotearoa New Zealand, this book will serve as a guide for social workers working with not just this community, but will contain important insights for working alongside many socially marginalised groups and communities.

To do this, this book contains an analysis of how older queer adults utilise social capital to develop relationships, connections, and access to social spaces. An understanding of social capital is an important resource in a social workers' toolset, as it can be used to understand the interactions between individuals and communities, alongside the resources and benefits that accrue as a result of those relationships, and we will apply that understanding to older queer community spaces in this book.

Supporting this analysis, in this book we consider how changes in legislation and social policy have, and importantly have not, impacted how older queer adults engage with social spaces. From legislative reform that includes – the decriminalisation of homosexuality and anti-discrimination protections to the development of social and civil equality laws in the form of civil unions and same-sex marriage – we will deconstruct the relationship between legislative reform that impacts the queer community, and how that influences how older queer adults navigate social spaces.

In order to move beyond potentially homogenous, or all-encompassing, conceptualisations of the queer community, we will address the specific ways in which access to broader queer spaces are contested and divided on the basis of identity, including, but not limited to, aspects such as sexuality, gender, and gender expression. In these narratives we will explore how some older queer adults have been excluded, or face discrimination, within queer spaces and communities. Building on this notion of exclusion, in this book we will specifically consider the ways age, and age-based stigma, impacts members of the queer community, critically assessing how space, community, and social environments are constructed and contested through an age-based lens.

Lastly, this book will consider how social work and other helping professionals can support older queer adults within social spaces at a micro, meso, and macro level. I aim to present to readers of this book insights, strategies, and reflections for using this content to inform their practice, learning, and teaching regarding social work with older adults in the queer community.

On "queering" language

The focus of this book is a group of people who have faced, and continue to face, cultural, political, and legal discrimination. As with any group of individuals who have been subject to prejudice, it is important to be careful and reflective with language that is used to refer to the community. For lesbian, gay, bisexual, transgender, queer, intersex, and asexual (LGBTQIA+) people, slurs and discriminatory language may have been used as a vehicle for social stigma and personal attacks. The impact of offensive or dismissive language can have long-lasting impacts, and the participants in my research were equally sensitive to the impact of stigmatising language:

> I am sensitive to homophobic comments that people make, and occasionally people will make a homophobic comment and I just jump down their throats. I just can't resist it. So I don't disclose sometimes, but I do tend to

come down heavily on people. Yeah, so I am sensitive
to those comments from people.

(Milly, 62)

The terms used to describe and identify with diverse sexual and gender identities have changed over time. Gay was once seen as a slur, but is now more commonly accepted; similarly queer has frequently been reappropriated to refer to diverse sexual and gender identities (Fox, 2007). In trying to define the LGBTQIA+ community, social science researchers have faced the challenge of summarising the diverse and varied experiences of each cohort. There are currently many conventions used to refer to this community, such as the LGBT, or more recently, the LGBTQ+ and LGBTQIA+ community. Other labels such as the queer or rainbow community are also used. These terms fit common social conventions and reflect the self-identification of LGBTQIA+ people and LGBTQIA+ communities (Cronin and King, 2010).

In this book I deliberately use the term queer when referring to broader LGBTQIA+ communities. This choice comes from the influence of queer theory on my own research and practice as a social worker. Queer theory supports a critique of binaries and discourses that focus on normative identities. Queer theory actively deconstructs categories of identity, as these categories often obscure differential experiences, and can have the by-product of reaffirming pre-existing inequalities (Fuss, 1991; Green, 2007). To apply queer theory, or to queer, is "to make strange, to frustrate, to counteract, to delegitimise, to camp up – heteronormative knowledge and institutions" (Sullivan, 2003, p. vi) – and the aim of this book is to challenge normative ideas of how older queer adults engage with social spaces. It is, as one participant mentioned to me in our interview, about giving language to lived reality:

> One of the things that has been very interesting to me when I did my own personal, very deep work around my identity, was absolutely no alternative language – there was just nothing outside the binary. That's lovely for me working now with young people, and there's a whole new language coming out of their exploration, their lived reality.
>
> (Rowan, 62)

In this book, I aim to recognise the diverse range of individuals who I interviewed, while also critically examining the heteronormative and cisnormative social structures that categorise them as minorities (Smith, Shin, and Officer, 2011). However, consistently referring to the participants as "queer" feels somewhat awkward due to the recruitment strategies I employed, which often used the terminology and language of "LGBTQIA+ communities" to connect with them. Furthermore, during the interviews, the participants themselves often used terms like gay, lesbian, and straight to describe themselves, others, and community groups.

Given these factors, I have taken the time to reflect on my choice of language and its relevance to both the participants and the research context. When discussing the individuals involved in this study as a whole or referring to the broader group of older adults who identify as lesbian, gay, bisexual, transgender, queer, intersex, or asexual I will use the term "queer" to encompass the diverse range of people it represents. Additionally, when discussing specific commonalities, exceptions, or experiences of different groups, I employ terms such as lesbian, gay, bisexual, transgender, queer, intersex, and asexual as appropriate. This approach respects the participants' self-identifications and ensures an accurate reflection of the stories they chose to share about their lived experiences and identities.

Aotearoa New Zealand

In addition to considering language, the context in which this research was conducted plays a crucial role in this book. The research took place in Aotearoa New Zealand (Aotearoa is the contemporary Māori name for New Zealand), where specific contextual factors influenced how participants responded to the questions and interviews. Aotearoa New Zealand has a troubled history regarding the treatment of sexual and gender diversity. When Aotearoa New Zealand became a British Colony in 1840, sexual activity between two men became illegal, and the punishment upon conviction was the death penalty. Later in 1867, the punishment was changed to life imprisonment. Although sex between two women was never illegal in Aotearoa New Zealand, non-heterosexual women still faced the negative impact of social stigma surrounding homosexual behaviour (Brickell, 2008).

Throughout this book, I examine various legislative and social policy developments that have shaped the experiences of older queer adults. These include the Homosexual Law Reform Act (1986), which decriminalised sexual activity between two men; the Human Rights Act (1993), which incorporated sexuality and gender into anti-discrimination legislation; and the Civil Unions Act (2004) and the Marriage (Definition of Marriage) Amendment Act (2013), which respectively recognised civil unions and same-sex marriage. I explore how these developments have impacted the broader queer community and critique contemporary Aotearoa New Zealand society for its treatment of older queer adults. While my aim is not to provide an exhaustive historical account of the experiences of the queer community throughout Aotearoa New Zealand history, the significance of these legislative changes is evident in the narratives and responses of the participants.

Interviews and participant narratives

At the core of this book are the stories, narratives, and experiences of the older queer adults I interviewed. These experiences are key to understanding how older queer adults engage with and access social spaces, and I wish for their insights to be the driving force of this exploration. Quotes and excerpts from these interviews will be used throughout the book, drawing attention to the experiences older queer adults have in social spaces. All participants were assigned a first-name pseudonym to protect their identity and privacy, and these pseudonyms are attached to each quote. I interviewed 31 older queer adults over the course of 12 months (2014–2015), travelling across Aotearoa New Zealand to interview people in their own homes, communities, and neighbourhoods. All the participants were over the age of 60 at the time of the interview, and all were navigating the process of ageing as an older queer person in a heteronormative and cisnormative society. The number following the participant pseudonyms indicates the age of the participant at the time of the interview. The participants I talked to all identified as queer, with a diverse range and intersection of sex, sexual identity, gender, and gender expression, and the pronouns used when discussing the participants experiences reflect their personal preference.

It is important to note at the beginning of this book that all the participants I interviewed identified as either Pākehā[2] or had immigrated from the United States or Europe. This is significant as Aotearoa New Zealand has a diverse population, with people from Europe, Asia, Africa, North and South America, and the Pacific region, alongside Māori as tangata whenua – the indigenous people of Aotearoa New Zealand. It would be expected that the narratives, experiences, alongside the social and community dynamics of the participants would vary significantly across the intersection of race and ethnicity. It was intended that this research would include a diverse range of participants, taking into account race, ethnicity, culture, and background. However recruitment efforts were unsuccessful in this endeavour, requiring a contextualisation of the findings and narratives in this book. While the narratives presented do represent a broad range of experiences from the queer community – primarily along the nexus of sexual identity, sexual characteristics, and gender – they cannot be unpacked through the intersection of race, ethnicity, and cultural background. As a result readers should be critical about assuming universal characteristics of the narratives, and consider how they might apply them to their own communities, cultures, and backgrounds.

After the interviews I analysed our conversations, drawing out findings, insights, and material that was relevant to my research question using the theoretical framework below. While I have aimed to present the material in this book as accessibly as possible, focusing on the participant stories first, and analysis second, this theoretical framework is important in understanding in how we can approach, interpret, and apply the findings from the participant narratives and stories.

Theoretical framework

This book is shaped by two theoretical lenses: critical social theory and critical gerontology. These lenses have some overlap as they are both broad and eclectic perspectives. However, I separate them to focus on the social structures of heteronormativity and cisnormativity, while also highlighting the significance of age and ageing in the life course. Heteronormativity is the assumption that a heterosexual orientation is the norm for human experiences (Willis et al., 2016). Similarly, cisnormativity refers to the assumption that a person's gender identity is the same as the sex they were assigned at birth, or matches socially assumed physical characteristics (Fenaughty and Pega, 2016). Both heteronormativity and cisnormativity privilege individuals who adhere to those social assumptions, while disadvantaging individuals who do not fit those standards. Alongside this theoretical framework, I utilise the concept of social capital to explore the connections between individuals, communities, and wider social structures. Social capital helps examine how social connectedness and the exchange of valuable resources can impact wellbeing. Although there are criticisms regarding the use of social capital in the social sciences, when combined with critical social theory and critical gerontology, it becomes a useful model for social work practice and research.

Critical social theory

Critical social theory is a broad term, encompassing a range of perspectives and approaches for examining social structures. While it does not refer to a single theoretical approach, it does provide guidelines for adopting a critical perspective in social work and social science research. Broadly, critical social theory has a variety of aims that are in line with social work goals. These goals include individual and community emancipation, highlighting forms of hidden coercion, and advocating for personal liberty (Guess, 1981).

Critical social theory requires both a perspective and a goal, as it challenges the notion of researchers as passive observers of social phenomena. Social workers adopting critical social theory aim to explore how cultural and political forces influence individual lives and communities. Through critiquing and exposing cultural forms of social constraints, the goal is to promote their recognition and rejection. This approach assumes that identifying and acknowledging power discrepancies is necessary before achieving change. It is a reflective and self-referential process, acknowledging that researchers and their research are not isolated entities, but are inherently connected and influence one another (see Figure 1.1).

Critical gerontology

Critical gerontology has played a significant role in shaping the theoretical framework of this book. It examines the ageing process, challenging socially constructed ideas of ageing and the social systems that impact individuals and communities as they age. Adopting critical gerontology in social work research involves evaluating the perception of age through

Examination of
social structures

Acknowledgement of
power and disadvantage

Rejection of
social binaries

Critique

Highlight oppression

Emphasise diversity
and subjectivity

**CRITICAL
SOCIAL THEORY**

**Critical social action, emancipation,
individual and community liberation**

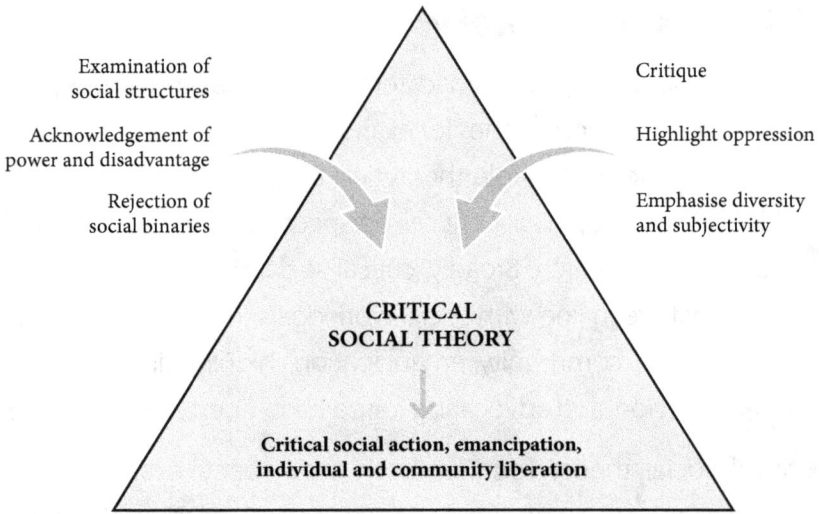

Figure 1.1 Critical social theory

physiological, sociological, political, and economic critiques. Critical gerontology encompasses two distinct lines of inquiry: a structural perspective and an individual perspective. Structural inquiry critiques the social, economic, and political forces that shape the ageing process, particularly how they intersect with ethnicity, socioeconomic status, sexuality, and gender. The individual line of inquiry focuses on personal experiences and individual diversity within the lives of older adults. These two lines of inquiry are interconnected in critical gerontological analysis and are central to interpreting the wellbeing of older queer individuals.

Critical gerontology challenges conventional dimensions of identity, such as the heterosexual/homosexual binary, providing a framework for emancipation from social and cultural dominance. It critiques formal and informal structures that support older

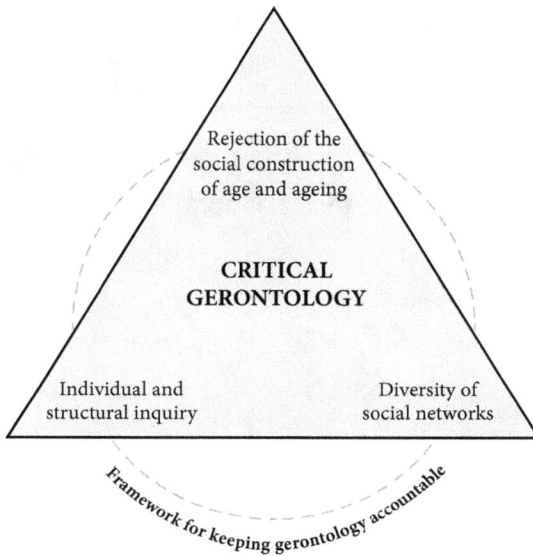

Figure 1.2 Critical gerontology

adults while incorporating overlapping perspectives on age, ethnicity, culture, sexuality, and gender identity (see Figure 1.2).

Social capital

This book also aims to explore how social capital influences the wellbeing of older queer adults. Social capital has been embraced by social workers as a flexible model for understanding the social connectedness of individuals and communities (Barker and Thomson, 2015; Fine, 2007; Healy and Hampshire, 2002). It originated as a critique of inflexible and unresponsive service delivery from government institutions, aiming to empower individuals and communities by enabling self-driven change, access to resources, and advocacy (Healy and Hampshire, 2002).

In this book, the terminology "social capital" aligns with the framework of bonding, bridging, and linking social capital

(Healy and Hampshire, 2002). Bonding social capital refers to connections among individuals within the same social sphere, while bridging social capital pertains to connections across different social spheres and communities. Linking social capital involves connections with external spheres that offer valuable resources (Barker and Thomson, 2015; Baum and Ziersch, 2003). The definition of valuable resources is subjective, varying across communities and individuals, encompassing economic, political, and social benefits. Previous research has identified valued resources as emotional and personal support, practical assistance, financial aid, specific knowledge and skills, and access to individuals with political or social power (Barker and Thomson, 2015; Blair and Carroll, 2008; Healy and Hampshire, 2002). Given the broad range of resources, this book focuses on contextual factors related to subjective wellbeing, allowing participants to define their own understanding of "valued resources" during the research interviews.

Social capital involves more than connections between individuals and communities. It necessitates the essential components of contact, resource exchange, and trust, obligation, and reciprocity (Barker and Thomson, 2015; Wilson, 2006). Merely having established relationships is not sufficient to qualify as social capital. I went beyond social connections in interviews and analysis to focus on perceptions of trust, reciprocity, and obligation, exploring how members of social capital networks perceive the receipt and provision of valued resources (see Figure 1.3).

The theoretical framework encompassing critical social theory, critical gerontology, and social capital provides the foundation

Individual
and community
benefits

The exchange
of valued
resources

Preconditions
of trust,
obligation, and
reciprocity

**SOCIAL
CAPTITAL**

Bonding,
bridging,
and linking
connections

Inclusion and
participation

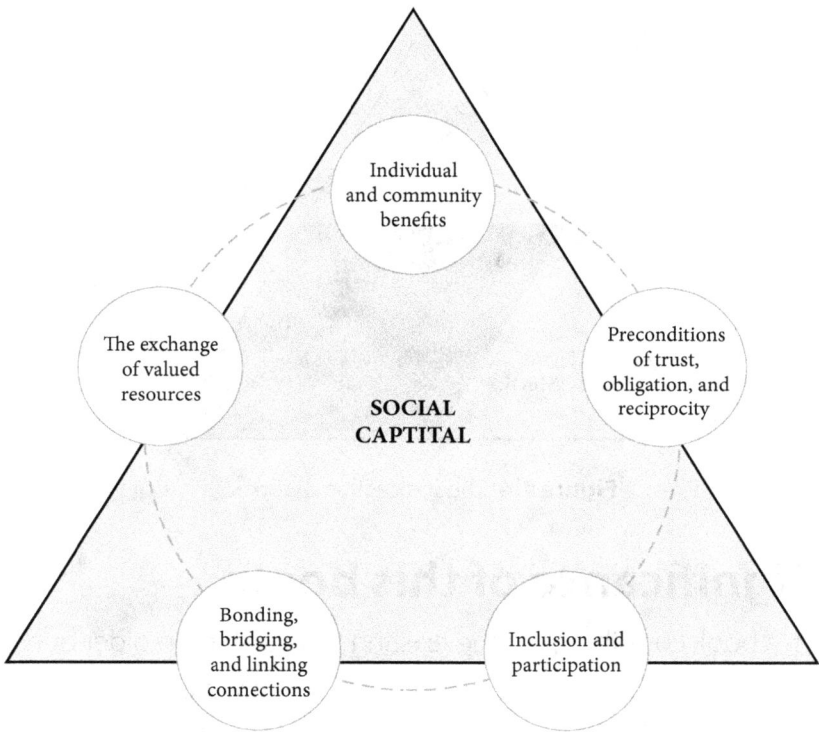

Figure 1.3 Social capital

for this book. Critical social theory and critical gerontology guided the interview questions, enabling an examination of the influence of social structures and forces on the lives of older queer individuals. The model of social capital necessitated an exploration of networks and relationships within communities, as well as the dynamics of closed social networks in relation to diverse identities. Each component, critical social theory, critical gerontology, and social capital, contributes equally to the theoretical framework of this book, as depicted in Figure 1.4.

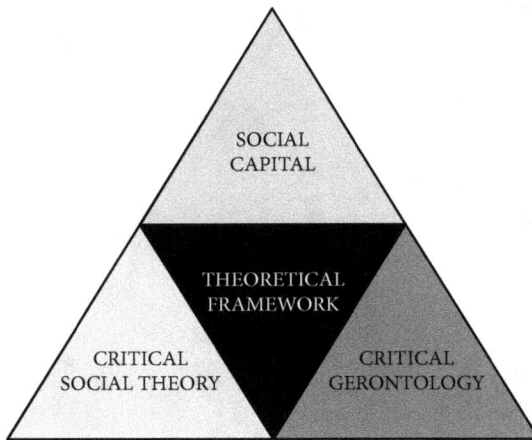

Figure 1.4 Theoretical framework

Significance of this book

This book contributes to the existing scholarship on older queer individuals and aims to inform social work practice, recognising the growing importance of supporting this population (Abendstern et al., 2012; Croghan, Moone, and Olson, 2014; Fredriksen-Goldsen et al., 2011; Hughes, Harold, and Boyer, 2011; Sharek, et al., 2015). The ageing population in Aotearoa New Zealand is increasing, with projections indicating a doubling of adults over the age of 65 by 2046 (Statistics New Zealand, 2013). This demographic shift can be seen across the world, and necessitates the preparedness of social work as a profession to support older adults, including those from diverse backgrounds and communities. It is crucial for social workers to possess the necessary knowledge and cultural sensitivity to effectively support older queer individuals, given their higher rates of poor mental health and previous experiences of inadequate social services (Croghan, Moone, and Olson, 2014; Fredriksen-Goldsen et al., 2011; Sharek et al., 2015). This understanding should be informed by an awareness of the diversity and lived experiences of older queer individuals at all levels of social work practice, policy, and education.

Book outline

This book is structured into eight chapters, each addressing different aspects of the experiences of older queer adults. Following this introductory Chapter 1, Chapter 2 focuses on specific forms of social capital highlighted by the participants and explores unique components of social capital for this population. Chapter 3 examines the impact of legislative and social policy changes in Aotearoa New Zealand on their engagement with social spaces. In Chapter 4, the multiple identities and relationships within the queer community are explored, including conflicts that arise in shared social spaces. Chapter 5 delves into the experiences of age and ageism, highlighting how older queer individuals often face exclusion from both mainstream society and the queer community due to their age. Chapter 6 investigates the interactions of older adults with health, social services, and aged care. Chapter 7 offers guidance to social workers on utilising the book's content to support the wellbeing and social inclusion of older queer adults. Finally, Chapter 8 concludes with reflections on the writing process, identifies future directions for social workers in this area, and advocates for reshaping and redefining social spaces to better accommodate older queer adults.

2
What is social about social capital?

Learning objective: to understand the concept of social capital within the context of older queer adults

By studying this chapter, readers will develop a clear understanding of social capital and its significance at interpersonal, community, and structural levels for older queer adults. They will explore the unique forms of social capital present within the queer community and the value attached to these connections.

Learning objective: to analyse the benefits and utilisation of social capital by older queer adults

Throughout this chapter, readers will examine how older queer adults utilise and engage with social capital to enhance their wellbeing and navigate various social environments. They will gain insight into the specific ways in which social capital operates within this population, including its benefits and the role it plays in supporting older queer adults.

Introduction

> The profound truth is you cannot be human on your
> own. You are human through relationship.
>
> (Archbishop Desmond Tutu, 2013)

Like Tutu's fundamental law quoted above, this book is focused on the interpersonal and community relationships of older queer adults, and how this impacts their ability to navigate social spaces. As described in Chapter 1, there is more to social capital than just relationships between individuals and communities. Most conceptualisations of social capital have highlighted that the preconditions of trust, obligation, and reciprocity between individuals are required (Pawar, 2006; Shortt, 2004; Wilson, 2006). Other writers have stressed that it is not just relationships that define social capital, but rather it is the access to, and sharing of, valued resources (Barker and Thomson, 2015; Healy and Hampshire, 2002). While the practice of using social capital to explore community networks has increased across the social sciences and the humanities over the last few decades, it is not free from criticism. Social capital has been critiqued for failing to account for the influences of class, power, and conflict, and is often measured through quantitative means, potentially ignoring the nuanced experiences that personal narratives and stories can provide (Fine, 2007; Pawar, 2006). Social capital is not a universally accepted model for exploring community spaces, but it can still provide a valuable insight into diverse and potentially invisible community connection – such as those used by older queer adults. In this chapter, I use the interviews I conducted to explore how social capital might be used by older queer adults to build relationships, navigate social spaces, and build supportive communities.

Social connectedness

Social capital is a resource that can benefit both individuals and communities, and it's often described in terms of the relationships between people and how those relationships can help communities thrive. When we talk about "connections" or "social connectedness," we're referring to the ways in which people connect with each other and participate in their communities. In this chapter, we'll be focusing on the ways in which older queer adults access and participate in their community, and we'll be exploring the common forms of social connectedness that emerged from the interviews. We'll start by looking at the community as a whole, and then we'll delve into the personal relationships that were particularly important for the participants' wellbeing and support.

Community

When we talk about "community" in the context of social capital for older queer adults, it can be a bit unclear what we mean. During the interviews, I intentionally left the term "community" undefined so that participants could interpret it in their own way. I didn't want to steer them towards a particular definition or limit their responses. This approach allowed for a diverse range of topics and examples to emerge, all related to the concept of community.

A lot of the study participants were able to maintain their connections with their community through networks formed around volunteering or providing services to others. For example, during one interview, Brian spoke at length about a program he worked for and how it helped others. He saw this as a prime example of how he engaged with his local community.

> It's the [*name of organisation*] and it goes into participating high schools every year and issues a survey to all of the year ten to establish which kids are at risk of failure, low self-esteem, and identifies the ten boys and the ten girls, who are most likely to benefit from their programme. And then they invite them and their parents and then they take them on a three-week wilderness challenge with specialist educators. And then they come back to town and they have a three-week community challenge. And then they have a mentor or one-on-one same-sex mentor for a year, and that mentor is like a big brother or big sister. It doesn't have a role of a parent or a teacher. They stand alongside them rather than above them or below them.
>
> (Brian, 65)

During the interview, Brian emphasised that being involved in his community and providing resources and support to others was crucial for his own wellbeing. He felt a sense of purpose and fulfilment in helping others, which in turn made him feel more connected to his community. For Brian, the act of giving back was not only important for the people he was helping, but also for his own mental and emotional health. In essence, he saw his involvement in the community as a two-way street, where both he and others benefited from his contributions.

> I think a lot of my sense of wellbeing over the years has come from feeling I'm useful, so that's why I continue to volunteer in things where I feel I can be useful and where I can use the skills, the training that I have in the 42 years of practice and education. That sort of thing.
>
> (Brian, 65)

This theme of community connection based on "giving back" or "providing support" for others was consistent throughout the interviews. During another interview, Isaac touched on similar themes:

> I've always belonged to groups that are a mixture of social and campaigning. It's always been an important thing to me, so a group that's only social I have much less interest in.
>
> (Isaac, 68)

Research with older adults has shown that volunteering and being active in community organisations can have benefits for both individuals and communities (Choi and Kim, 2011; Narushima, 2005; Theurer and Wister, 2010). Older adults tend to be the most dedicated volunteers, motivated by sympathy, altruism, and a sense of social responsibility (Choi and Kim, 2011). The interviews conducted for this study highlighted the strong influence of social responsibility on the participants.

While many participants in this study found a sense of community connectedness by providing formal support and resources to others, not all reflections were solely focused on this aspect. Some participants identified groups and organisations that they actively engaged with, which provided them with a sense of personal wellbeing. These groups included both queer organisations and groups open to the general population. For instance, Alexander elaborated on his involvement with various community groups that gave him connections and relationships in the community:

> I have social connections through the Rainbow Club for gay friends, and I've been a member of that for, well since 2005, so a few years now. It's been ten years I've been a member of the Rainbow Club and knowing all the people there. So I have those social connections. As far as community groups and stuff, I'm in choir. I guess you make contacts through swimming. I go swimming pretty much every day or the gym – not often enough obviously – but I do make social connections through that. So I have connections in the community.
>
> (Alexander, 63)

During the interviews, another participant shared his experience about the support they received from community connections following a relationship break-up. Andrew spoke about the unique resources that a queer-friendly group could provide in such situations, especially in contexts where many social groups were not open to queer people:

> On the gay side it is mainly the Gay Dads' Group and the Rainbow Group. Although I belong to them, it's not exclusively – I belong to about 15 or 16 different organisations, from Progressive Association to the St Vincent de Paul Society to the Hall Committees – but mainly community-based. My main contact initially was through the Gay Dads' Group, because in those days, in

the 1980s, it was just when the law change was being mooted when I became aware of my sexuality, and it caused the break-up of my family. I got tremendous assistance from them, and they're still going, but now it's just a social group where we meet once a month and have a shared dinner. But in those days it really was essential to have somebody that could tell you who a gay-friendly lawyer would be and how to go about some of the problems you had in your daily life.

(Andrew, 80)

For many participants, community was closely tied to giving back to others and engaging with political movements. Having access to a variety of community connections is a fundamental aspect of social capital, as it has been shown to increase quality of life, wellbeing, and social empowerment (Talo, Mannarini, and Rochira, 2014). However, close personal connections also played an essential role in developing social capital for the participants.

Close friends and chosen family

The notion of "close personal relationships" covers a broad range of personal connections, from long-time friends, partners, and romantic relationships to both close and wider family networks. As with the concept of community connectedness, what constitutes a personal relationship was left open during the interviews for the participants to interpret. One of the more consistent themes to emerge from the interviews was the emphasis placed on close personal friendships.

Part of the importance placed on close friends by the participants was the reality that many acted as their "family of choice." In many situations it was this family of choice that was identified as the primary support network of the participants – and therefore was crucial to their wellbeing:

> I've got a really good network of friends support in the States. Which is a mixed bag of gays and straights and just everyone, they're all very close. And I said to them, I said that was one of the things I missed when I came to New Zealand, initially, especially, was that closeness and they went well "you'll have friends." And I went "yeah, but you guys are kind of more than friends – you're actually like a family. If someone's ill, or something, you get together probably two or three times a month for meals and stuff, so it's more like a family."
>
> (Alexander, 63)

Alexander's story highlights how valuable close connections, and a family of choice, are for older queer adults. It provided a sense of closeness, support, and belonging. This was particularly stressed as Alexander moved to Aotearoa New Zealand later in life, and as highlighted above was primarily concerned about losing this network of friends in the US. Luckily Alexander was able to build a new network upon arriving in Aotearoa New Zealand, and he elaborated further on the impact of a family of choice, noting not only the practical benefits of such a group, but also the emotional support they provided for each other:

> A whole group of friends that don't physically live together but we're in close enough physical proximity that if someone becomes ill or care is needed, we all take care of that person. Generally we're thinking along

that line. It doesn't have to be until they die, but if they do, and then move on until the last one's standing kind of thing. But I think that that's what we've agreed would be a good common goal for the future, so there's some care. Because none of us have this large group of family, so, especially I think with a lot of gay friends. They don't really have any. They're old or their parents are not living obviously and they don't have children, some of them, and maybe they don't have good relationships, or don't have siblings. So basically they rely on other friends and stuff who are like family. Nothing is set in stone – we don't have any written contracts – but I think that's the agreed upon thing that we'll do as we get older, is just take care of each other.

(Alexander, 63)

Previous research (Hughes and Heycox, 2010) has also shown that older queer adults tend to rely more on close personal friends than their biological families. This emphasises the uniqueness of social capital networks for older queer adults compared to older heterosexual individuals. Since they have fewer potential connections due to their limited reliance on parents, siblings, or children, their accessible support is also reduced. Thus, the participants in this study emphasised the crucial role of close friends in their wellbeing as they often act as their family of choice.

During the discussions around family of origin versus family of choice, an interesting theme emerged related to the terminology used by participants. They used the term "family" to describe people they could rely on for support, who formed a close network and provided the basis for a large number of social capital resources. Although the term "family of choice" is commonly used to refer to these networks in academic literature, the use of the term "family" raises questions about how it is defined and used in practice. This brings up questions such as who defines family, what does it mean, and what are the criteria for it? These considerations have important implications for social work practice, social services systems, and social policy. Since "family" typically refers to a narrow band of experiences, primarily a biological and nuclear family, this raises concerns about how older queer adults may be affected when they come across these services and define and use the idea of family differently.

Despite previous research suggesting that older queer adults are less likely to have familial support (Antonelli and Dettore, 2014; Hughes and Kentlyn, 2011), a significant number of participants in this study did have access to family members, including adult children and grandchildren. This is notable given that previous research has highlighted the lower likelihood of queer adults having children (Fredriksen-Goldsen et al., 2013), and it may be due to the possibility that some queer adults felt more comfortable coming out after the Homosexual Law Reform (1986) was passed, potentially leaving partners who already had children.

While some participants in the study had children, not all had positive relationships with them. For those who did have positive relationships with their children, they found them to be a dependable source of support and social capital, as Sue discussed with me:

> Both of my children who live in Christchurch have …
> at my age and my physical condition … I had a knee

replacement and I went and stayed with my daughter after that. I stayed with her for three weeks. And I stayed with her after one carpal tunnel operation for a couple of weeks. My son and his wife, I had a godawful shit of an experience last October. I got an infection in my knee replacement and it was cut open and scraped out and then two days later it was cut open and scraped out again. Wound up being in public hospital for a month, at Burwood Rehab for a month, and then I went and stayed at my son's place for about three weeks and learned how to walk again. So it is reciprocal.

(Sue, 75)

While some of the participants in the study had positive relationships with their children, there were also accounts of strained relationships. James, for instance, shared his experience of being cut out of his life by his adopted son after the latter discovered his sexual orientation. James' experience sheds light on the complexities of family relationships and how they can be affected by differences in sexual orientation or other factors. This highlights the importance of acknowledging the diversity of family structures and the need for support networks beyond traditional family units:

I had a son – I adopted him. My wife was married before. I came on the scene when [he] was 18 months old. We married when he was three, so he's only ever known me as his father. Anyway, he is now in a relationship, he's got two children, two girls he's got – I've never seen them. He has changed his surname and reverted

to his birth father's name. He's totally homophobic, and
so therefore we have zero contact.

(James, 70)

Fraught family relationships can have a negative impact on
the wellbeing of older queer adults, as seen in James' situation.
Being estranged from a child not only brings emotional
consequences but also affects the support network they can
rely on. James' disconnection from his son has resulted in the
loss of contact with his grandchildren, further reducing his
wider network. Moreover, fractured relationships can disrupt
relationships with other people involved, such as shared
friends and family members. This rejection based on their queer
identity can lead to emotional hardship and loss of potential
supports, as well as a divided social network for older queer
adults, all negatively impacting the social capital available for
older queer adults.

Trusting relationships

In my interviews with older queer adults, I gained valuable
insights into the key elements of social capital that they valued in
their relationship and connections. The participants emphasised
the crucial role that trust and reciprocity play in their personal
and community connections. However, for these individuals, the
significance of trust was shaped by various contextual factors
likely to influence members of the queer community. Growing
up during a time of marginalisation and discrimination, including
prior to and during Homosexual Law Reform (1986) and the
Human Rights Act (1993), meant that trust was fundamental to
feeling socially connected with others. One participant, Liam,

illustrated this when he spoke about his close friend and primary confidant.

Liam: He is a very, very important person in my life. We met about 20 years ago. They've been a great friend all those two decades. Jamie is quite a remarkable person, a very brave person, and I think probably the one person I could say absolutely anything to.

David: So it's a very close personal relationship between the two of you?

Liam: With deep, deep trust, David. We wouldn't have that without trust, and knowing what we've gone through, I need that.

(Liam, 68)

The significance of trust in fostering community connectedness was not limited to personal connections alone. Melissa's experiences following the 2010 and 2011 Ōtautahi Christchurch (Ōtautahi is the contemporary Māori name for Christchurch) earthquakes exemplified the critical role of trust in building a sense of community among individuals. In the aftermath of the disaster, many people were displaced from their homes and communities, leaving them feeling isolated and vulnerable. Melissa shared how, during this difficult time, the trust that people placed in one another was essential in establishing a sense of connection and support. People came together to offer assistance, resources, and emotional support, creating a sense of community that might not have otherwise existed. Melissa's experience highlights how trust can be a powerful tool for fostering social connections, even in the most challenging circumstances:

> The whole neighbourhood after the earthquake. It's a really good example, actually, of our community. Our sleep-out flooded. Of course, we're red-zoned so everybody's been in limbo. It was just on a concrete slab that cracked, so neighbours offered and another neighbour lent them the jacks to jack up the thing. Another neighbour did the levels. We'd go out to work – I think we were both working – and come home and just find the next stage. But it was like you could totally trust them. And it was a real community effort.
>
> (Melissa, 64)

Trust appears to play a crucial role in the formation of social capital among older queer adults, given the high frequency of hostile encounters experienced by this population. As Dylan pointed out, incidents of homophobia and discrimination are unfortunately all too common for older queer adults, and can contribute to feelings of isolation and disconnection:

> I prefer to live by myself, because I don't trust other people. After what I've been through in my life I don't trust anyone.
>
> (Dylan, 73)

Trust plays a central role in strengthening connections among older members of the queer community, supporting wellbeing and reducing anxiety about the behaviour of others. However, measuring and defining trust has its limitations. It has been argued that trust is temporary and fades once relationships with strangers become established, becoming embedded in practices of reciprocity (Torche and Valenzuela, 2011). However, the discussions I had with the participants did not support this distinction, as trust and reciprocity were commonly linked for older queer adults. While it may be possible to theoretically separate the two in discussions about social capital, for this population, trust remained an integral factor even when reciprocal exchanges of resources began. This highlights the importance of trust as a foundation for building and maintaining supportive relationships, particularly in the face of discrimination and marginalisation. By recognising the significance of trust in promoting social capital among older queer adults, we can better understand and support the diverse and complex social networks that sustain this community.

Reciprocity in action

During the interviews, participants often discussed the concept of reciprocity when talking about their relationships. Unlike trust, which was seen as a more abstract idea, many participants spoke about the intentional give and take involved in reciprocal relationships. They described the practicalities of offering support and assistance to one another, such as providing transportation or companionship. For instance, Hannah spoke about a close friend who helped her out by giving her lifts to medical appointments.

> The reciprocity there is that she hasn't got a car so I take her places and provide her with friendship in the form of a listening. So that's that reciprocity.
>
> (Hannah, 72)

While, on the topic of financial support, Mark discussed supporting his sister:

> I think that I've been a support for her. She had a pretty rough time as a consequence of the earthquakes, and over the years she has run into financial problems and I've helped her with that. So we've been reasonably mutually supportive towards each other.
>
> (Mark, 75)

The participants consistently emphasised the importance of reciprocity in their relationships. Reciprocity, for them, was a way of exchanging resources, and is a key component of social capital, which views networks and connections as a means for individuals and communities to access valuable resources. The exchange of emotional support was a significant example of reciprocity in the relationships of the participants, highlighting the important role it played in their lives:

> For the early part of my life I was involved in what I would say now were some very violent relationships – the relationships were not healthy, I didn't have a framework for knowing what a healthy relationship was then. And so, once I learned that about myself and owned it, I've been pretty particular with the people who are my friends. They're high-functioning people, and I think it would be very fair to say that we as a group of people love each other, and that it flows both ways. So yes, sometimes you're supporting friends through tough times, and other times they're supporting you through tough times, so it's very mutual.
>
> (Rowan, 62)

However not all relationships were characterised by reciprocity, which was a source of frustration for some of the participants.

Hannah acknowledged that situational factors could influence the level of support that individuals could offer, and discussed a personal example of a close friend who did not respond in a way that Hannah felt was expected or deserved. This highlights that while reciprocity is an important aspect of social capital, it is not always guaranteed in every relationship:

> Intermittent, depending on what's going on in whose lives. Yeah, what they're dealing with. But sometimes it goes the other way, doesn't it, obviously.
>
> (Hannah, 72)

Others were more likely to express dissatisfaction with the state of their relationships if their perceived level of reciprocity was not met:

> I've got to go in for an eye operation the beginning of next month and I've asked him, would he drive me there, cos I can't drive home. And he said yes, but now he's humming and harring [sic] about it, and I said – I don't know how I can manage to do it without him, but I suppose I could ask my son. He doesn't like being put out. He just thinks about himself. And it annoys me a bit, because I'm always available for other people. So it pisses me off if they're not available for me.
>
> (Benjamin, 76)

Reciprocity plays a significant role in the development of social capital by promoting mutual expectations and benefits between individuals. Those who fulfil the expectations of reciprocal relationships can benefit from increased social capital. Conversely, individuals who violate these expectations may experience a hindrance in their social capital development, as shown by the frustrations expressed by Benjamin.

Exchange of resources

To build social capital, networks and their members must create different kinds of resources that can meet individual and collective needs (Baum and Ziersch, 2003). However, most social capital theories primarily consider financial goods and services (Blair and Carroll, 2008), which has drawn criticism from social science experts (Mohan and Mohan, 2002). This book, on the other hand, focuses on alternative aspects of social capital. While financial support was mentioned by participants as a potential outcome of social connections, the main emphasis in the interviews was on the significance of emotional support.

Emotional and personal support

The participants in this book emphasised that the most significant outcome of social capital was its ability to facilitate the exchange of emotional and personal support. Throughout various interviews, it was observed by the participants that their social connections within communities and with other individuals directly and indirectly offered emotional support. Some of these conversations specifically highlighted the concept of passive emotional support, as described by Beth:

> It's just somebody there to be able to talk to. You can be sitting in silence, but if you want to say something, there's something to say. You know that – comfortable. Like a pair of old shoes that fit well. So yeah – that's about it. It's just somebody there, who's comfortable

to be with, and who cares about what happens to me, and I care about what happens to her. So yeah, we look after each other.

(Beth, 65)

Frequently, the participants emphasised that the ability to unload and express their emotions played a crucial role in how emotional support was both given and received:

Oh yeah, absolutely. But also that I can tell them all the dreadful stuff. I can offload stuff too. To some friends I can offload all the really awful stuff that's going on for me. And I think that's really important, to have that space with friends where you can just hang it out really, yeah, yeah.

(Hannah, 72)

Furthermore, a significant number of participants were able to engage in detailed discussions about the reciprocal nature of emotional support exchange. They shared experiences of offering empathetic listening, providing reassurance, and offering a safe space for others to express their emotions. These conversations shed light on the dynamic and interactive nature of emotional support within their social networks. Participants recognised that emotional support was not a one-way street but rather a mutual exchange that fostered a sense of connectedness and strengthened interpersonal bonds:

Oh, yes, yes, you get a lot out of it. When you put any energy into anything – as you know, too, when you visit your people that have got their problems, you get far more love back out of it.

(Andrew, 80)

One important function of this emotional support for the participants was to hold each other accountable in ways that were not possible in less personal relationships. Michelle specifically highlighted this aspect, stating:

Yes, she's always been someone I can talk through things with. If something's bothering me or if I've been ill, she's been incredibly supportive. She's not afraid to tell me what I should do differently than what I do. She doesn't live in awe of me. I think we have quite an equal sort of friendship and she is a wise woman, and I respect that about her.

(Michelle, 73)

During one interview, a participant openly shared his personal journey with mental health and emphasised the crucial role of emotional support provided by a close friend. This support involved the friend helping him recognise and break free from cycles of negative thinking. Benjamin articulated this experience by stating:

There was one very good friend of mine, for 30-odd years he was a friend – never a sexual friend, although he was gay and had his own partner. But we were more like brothers in the finish, and I could always go to him and say, you know, and he would never say "get over it." He would point out flaws in my thinking.

(Benjamin, 76)

The participants in this book emphasised the significance of emotional support as a valuable resource due to its relationship with overall wellbeing. In various ways, they expressed an awareness that emotional support contributed to their overall sense of wellbeing. Wellbeing theories, encompassing elements such as positive emotion, social engagement, self-assessed meaning, positive relationships, and accomplishment (Seligman, 2011), align with the multifaceted nature of emotional support identified in this book. The close personal and community connections that served as sources of emotional support were highly cherished by the participants. The presence of close personal and community connections offering this valued resource indicated that the participants were recognised and accepted by others, providing another layer of support and fostering the development of wellbeing.

It is important to note that this by-product of emotional support may not be universally experienced by all members of the queer community, as it might specifically reflect the experiences of older queer adults who have faced decades of discrimination and social stigma. Nevertheless, it underscores the need to consider the nuances and diverse experiences that different communities may encounter when assessing the value of social capital.

Practical support

Emotional support was just one aspect of the resources that were generated and exchanged within the social capital networks of older queer adults. While discussing their reliance on others, many of the participants also emphasised the practical assistance they received for their day-to-day tasks. In their accounts, several participants highlighted how their social capital provided access to individuals with diverse skill sets or physical capabilities that were helpful in fulfilling various tasks. A participant shared an example involving his flatmates, illustrating how their unique skills complemented one another:

> Well, really it's the four of us and we have different skills. Pete spends most of the weekend on a tractor going around cutting the lawns and weeding and things like that, whereas Kevin doesn't like the outdoors much at all. He's a big film buff and [city] in particular is much better for film than we experienced even living in large cities in Yorkshire.
>
> (Isaac, 68)

An additional participant shared her experience of relying on her partner's sons for practical tasks, all while recognising the mutual reciprocity that existed within their relationship:

> Well, if I need anything done, I would ask my two sons. I say two, because they're kind of like sons, both of them. In the line of having my computer fixed, I would ask my sons. In the line of having things done around the house I'd ask them, cos there are obviously things I can't do. And on the other way round "oh Mum, won't you come and babysit this week?" "Yeah, sure." So I do a lot of babysitting.
>
> (Beth, 65)

The participants in this book engaged in a wide range of contexts where practical support and assistance were exchanged. Some participants recounted instances involving household tasks or providing help with childcare, while others shared stories that necessitated more extensive support. For instance, Mark was able to offer practical assistance to both his mother and sister during his mother's illness:

> When my mother was in her last few years, my youngest sister, she took the major role in caring for her, but it was me that would give her the relief from that. So I'd go down for periods of time when she needed a break, and live with my mother to support her, because she couldn't live alone. Yeah, and when I think about it, I have provided her quite a bit of support over the years. It's not needed at the moment, but when it has been needed.
>
> (Mark, 75)

While conventional conceptualisations of social capital often refer to resources exchanged within social networks using the language of goods and services, this chapter has taken a distinct approach by focusing on the qualitative understanding of what constitutes a "resource." The participants openly contemplated the pivotal role of emotional support in their personal and community connections. Moreover, they recognised that accessing practical support was often intertwined with emotionally supportive relationships, illustrating the interconnectedness between different forms of support.

Conclusion

The goal of this chapter was to examine what social capital means for older queer adults. A particular focus was how social capital may have unique components for older queer adults, and what historical and contemporary factors may have shaped their social capital. Beyond that, this chapter also aimed to highlight the more common forms of social connectedness expressed by participants, and discussed the idea of valued resources as they pertain to queer adults.

The narratives and experiences shared by the participants suggest that while trust and reciprocity are considered as foundational components of social capital, for older queer adults their roles are amplified. Trust was crucial in the development of relationships and was often founded on the need to be fully open about personal sexual or gender identities. Similarly, reciprocity helped cement and strengthen established relationships, potentially reducing the participants' stress or worries about future support. Part of the heightened emphasis on trust and reciprocity was because the participants had lived through a time of discrimination and stigma regarding social attitudes towards sexual and gender identities – both before and after changes in Aotearoa New Zealand legislation – meaning that trust in another person and the reciprocal exchange of support were vital to ensuring wellbeing.

Though valued resources can imply a wide range of different supports, goods, or services, for the participants in this research, it was emotional and personal support that they highlighted as the most important part of their social capital. Emotional support helped to assist the participants during times of stress, ill-health, bereavement, and also supported the general wellbeing of the participants. Aside from emotional support, the participants were quick to provide examples of practical support.

This particular form of support was related more to their own ability and competency – noting on occasion their inability to complete certain tasks due to age-related factors, or that they were able to rely on someone else with more information and specific skill sets. While not as strongly related to wellbeing as emotional support, these resources did aid participant wellbeing by assisting them to remain independent and free from extra stressors.

3
Swings and roundabouts

Shifts in policy, attitudes, and discrimination

Learning objective: to analyse the impact of changes in social policy on the lives of older queer adults

After studying this chapter, readers will be able to evaluate the impact of changes in laws and policies on the social attitudes and experiences of older queer adults. They will develop an understanding of how policy shifts have influenced the ways in which older queer adults navigate social spaces and engage with their communities.

Learning objective: to understand the importance of personal narratives in understanding the lived experiences of older queer adults

By engaging with this chapter, readers will be able to recognise the value of personal stories and perspectives from older queer adults. They will explore historical and present-day experiences to gain insight into the intersection of social policy, social attitudes, and the lives of older queer adults.

Introduction

> You're looking into Hades, you're looking at the homosexuals, don't look too hard you might catch AIDS – Norman Jones, National Party MP, 1985
>
> (Moir, 2016)

In 1985, comments like this were frequently directed at the queer community in Aotearoa New Zealand. At the time many people, including Members of Parliament (MP) like Norman Jones, were opposed to the passing of the Homosexual Law Reform Act in 1986. If passed, this Act would legalise sexual relationships between two men. Such was the extent of Jones' feeling on the matter, he was recorded as saying:

> Go back into the sewers where you come from … let all the normal people stand up … we do not want homosexuality legalised. We don't want our children contaminated by those people – Norman Jones, National Party MP, 1985
>
> (Moir, 2016)

The Homosexual Law Reform Act (1986) did pass, and it was one of several successful legislative Acts that aimed to promote the rights and safety of the queer community in Aotearoa New Zealand. However, it was not the end of public and private displays of bigotry. This chapter examines the idea that creating protective and inclusive social policies for older queer adults does not eliminate discriminatory or hostile social attitudes, like those mentioned by Norman Jones. Acknowledging this disconnection is important for social work to grapple with, and it directly informs how older queer adults engage with, and are supported by, social spaces.

Social work as a profession aims to promote social cohesion, empowerment, and the liberation of people (International Federation of Social Workers, 2023). It is this mandate that underpins practice, research, and social advocacy. A key perspective I am drawing from in this chapter is that for older queer adults the process of working towards social inclusion and acceptance is ongoing. It is important to note the positive developments around queer rights within Aotearoa New Zealand – from the decriminalisation of homosexuality, the development of anti-discrimination legislation, to the Marriage Amendment Act 2013 – however the experiences of the queer community present a different picture. A picture that still includes discrimination, abuse, and exclusion. As a result, a prominent theme in this chapter is that the impact of social policy is not immediately reflected in societal attitudes and behaviour. For older queer adults this means that the efforts of social policy to be inclusive and promote liberation are not necessarily felt on a day-to-day level – resulting in a complex relationship between legislative change and social development. For social workers, understanding this relationship is crucial because it helps us fulfil our professional duty to challenge laws that control and suppress marginalised communities.

Older queer adults have a unique historical and social background that allows them to reflect on the positive and negative effects of legislative changes related to their community. As "witnesses to dramatic, rapid, and ongoing social change in the construction of minority sexual and gender identity" (Van Wagenen, Driskell, and Bradford, 2013, p. 1), this position provides these older adults with a distinct perspective on queer rights, wellbeing, and inclusion. This unique perspective comes from a combination of shared experiences, including belonging to the queer community; exposure to minority stress, marginalisation; and the emergence of queer pride and resistance. However, it is important to not only highlight the concerns of older queer adults who fear being excluded from social spaces, but to equally explore stories of hope that things will improve and change over time. These narratives demonstrate the significant resilience that older queer adults have in the face of oppressive or dismissive social structures. A triumph, as Hannah mentioned to me during our interview, of hope:

> It was a triumph of hope. Maybe hope over experience. Mind you, that was the '60s ...
>
> (Hannah, 72)

This chapter centres on reconciling this hope with the understanding that progressive legislative reform alone cannot immediately bring about positive social change. The chapter is divided into several sections, which address the impact of legislative reform, the persistence of stigma and risk, the need for inclusivity, and the advancement of the sexual citizenship of older queer adults. Although there have been many advances for the queer community in Aotearoa New Zealand in recent decades, there is still progress to be made. Despite the offensive and bigoted views of individuals like Norman Jones, who archaically compared the queer community to Hades as quoted at the start of this chapter, queer rights have continued to improve. However, this chapter focuses on the stories and reflections from older queer adults who demonstrate that there is still work to be done to fully overcome societal barriers and improve access to social spaces.

Legislative change, visibility, and safety

During my interviews a significant topic was the impact of changes in Aotearoa New Zealand's laws on social attitudes towards the queer community. The stories and narratives shared by the participants highlighted a shift not only in legislation concerning sexual and gender identities but also in their own expectations of social life and social spaces. According to one participant, the experience of "coming out" or of disclosing and being open about their sexual identity, started to change leading up to and following Homosexual Law Reform (1986).

> Oh, you never really "come out" – oh you do, you come out over a long period of time until just about everybody knows. I started when I was in my early

twenties, when I was still at university, but probably the main part of it followed the 1986 law.

(Brian, 65)

Although Brian had previously felt at ease sharing his sexuality in specific circumstances, it was the enactment of the Homosexual Law Reform Act in 1986 that greatly affected his inclination and capability to be open in various settings. The passing of this legislation had a clear impact on how Brian revealed his sexuality and how it was perceivable to others. Nonetheless, this did not imply that he was now immune to discrimination. In fact, Brian proceeded to discuss the repercussions of coming out in his professional life and whether it had any bearing on his career.

> At that stage I was head of department in a large suburban co-ed school, and I thought, shit, they can know now, and so, they did. People ask "do you think you may have missed out on some promotions or opportunities because of it?" And I don't know. I know people who did. Sometimes I think so.

(Brian, 65)

As previously stated by Brian, although it may have appeared more secure to reveal one's sexuality in various settings, such as the workplace, this did not imply that legislative reform had entirely safeguarded the queer community from discriminatory treatment or reduced social prospects. In the workplace, this could manifest in missed promotions, isolation from office camaraderie, or even harassment from co-workers. Despite the reform, some of the participants believed that it had not provided them with adequate liberty to be truthful about their sexuality at work, considering the limited legal protections offered by it:

If I'd come out overtly gay when I was working in that senior position, I would never have been able to stay there. I would have been pushed aside.

(Mark, 75)

Mark elaborated on the challenges of holding a senior position, despite the implementation of the law reform. He drew links between societal attitudes towards individuals who identify as homosexual, and the expectations placed upon individuals in leadership roles:

At work it just was not possible, being in a senior position, to share being gay with somebody. You had to hide that. I think in those days, if you didn't scare the horses, nobody cared too much about what was going on. If nobody else had to put up with your overt sexuality, it didn't matter to people. So, my behaviour, on the outside, was always pretty straight.

(Mark, 75)

Mark's comment highlights a crucial issue regarding the intersection of legislation and social attitudes, which reveals that the mere passing of a law does not necessarily translate into the elimination of discrimination at an individual level. Despite legal changes intended to protect the rights of queer individuals, many still experience bias, prejudice, and intolerance in their daily lives, as social attitudes towards these communities continue to lag behind legal protections. Nonetheless, it is important to note that for some individuals, the legislative reform has had a positive impact on their lives, granting them a sense of confidence and security in openly expressing their queer identity:

I'm happier being this way than I was before. Yeah. I don't hide anything now. I don't have to. You could say what you like. Especially with the law change.

(Benjamin, 76)

The narratives present in this chapter about the Homosexual Law Reform Act (1986) demonstrate the intricate ways in which legislation can affect inner reflections and evaluations about disclosing sexual identities in social spaces. Unfortunately, the process of decriminalisation has not necessarily transformed the experiences of older queer adults.

Social stigma and risk

The impact of stigma in social spaces, and the subsequent risk of exclusion, violence, and discrimination, for older queer adults should be of concern to social workers. A useful framework for understanding the impact of this stigma is the concept of a hostile world scenario. The hostile world scenario refers to instances where marginalised individuals face constant threats, or perceived threats, to their physical and mental integrity (Shenman and Shmotkin, 2016). The impact of these constant threats – whether they are from physical harm, social isolation, or an inability to express an identity – have a significant impact on the wellbeing and social connections of older members of the queer community (Meyer, 2003). Although some of the participants reflected on how the decriminalisation of homosexuality led to an improvement in their self-confidence and feelings of safety, it was usually regarded as not having a significant impact on the views or values of the broader heteronormative community:

Yeah. So … it didn't remove the social stigma, but it did remove the legislative stigma. The risk. And I'd lived in France for three years, where being gay's never been outlawed, but where the social stigma was just as strong as here. So I could see that having no law against it was no guarantee of it being accepted by society.

(Brian, 65)

In 1986, the Homosexual Law Reform Act was passed, decriminalising consensual sex between men aged 16 and over in Aotearoa New Zealand. However, while sexual relationships between women were never technically illegal, they still faced discrimination, social stigma, and abuse while in same-sex relationships. According to Fenaughty and Pega, in Aotearoa New Zealand the "long-standing statutory discrimination and criminalisation of men served to significantly marginalise and obscure the needs of gender and sexually diverse minorities for many years to come," including women, transgender people, and non-binary individuals (2016, p. 229). As an example, during the time period where homosexual law reform was being debated, Michelle revealed that they experienced active and public social abuse simple for being in a relationship with another woman:

My first relationship with a woman, I was in Auckland Airport one day, it was probably my first personal experience. The relationship, it was clear, was just ending and like most of us, no matter whether we're in a heterosexual or a same-sex relationship, the ending of a first relationship in particular is pretty traumatic. And so we were both at the airport: I was going home and I was crying and crying and these two guys just started circling around and around just going "Dirty dykes. Dirty dykes."That was back in 1986.

(Michelle, 73)

The prevalence of abuse directed towards the queer community is why many of the people I talked to emphasised a need for greater legal protection following Homosexual Law Reform (1986). Therefore the inclusion of sexuality as a protected characteristic under the Human Rights Act (1993) was a significant turning point for many individuals who identified as queer in Aotearoa New Zealand. It instilled a sense of security and belonging that was previously lacking and provided a framework legally responding to discrimination and prejudice. Brian exemplified this sentiment when he acknowledged the positive impact that the Human Rights Act (1993) had on his personal life. He emphasised how the Act has contributed to the overall wellbeing and safety of the queer community, making it easier for individuals to assert their rights and live without fear of discrimination.

So the second plank of the platform was that anti-discrimination ... well, which didn't come through until '93. And that's when you could start complaining on the basis of explicit discrimination.

(Brian, 65)

However, there was an acknowlededgment that including sexuality within the Human Rights Act (1993) as a protected characteristic would not guarantee an end to discrimination, as it was noted that simply enacting legislation alone without promoting education and the normalisation of queer rights and queer experiences would not be effective:

I can see so many things identical to what was happening to me when I was growing up. And here we are, the law has changed, it's all legal and everything blah blah blah, but it's a load of "crap," because education hasn't come along. It hasn't come along with the legality side of it. That is the most annoying thing – and it was annoying right from day one.

(Dylan, 73)

During my research, I noticed that many people, including Dylan, were frustrated by the slow pace of social change and acceptance, despite progress being made through legislation. However, the older queer adults I spoke with shared their belief that social policy could promote greater social inclusion and participation, which would help legitimise their experiences, even if it did not necessarily increase their immediate safety.

Inclusivity and participation

A theme that was consistent across my interviews was the importance of being visible and included in society – where older queer adults would not have their rights and level of citizenship restricted along any axis of sexuality or gender identity (Richardson, 2017). Supporting this focus on the nature of sexual citizenship, a number of the conversations addressed the social and cultural significance of the Civil Union Act (2004) and the Marriage (Definition of Marriage) Amendment Act (2013). Tom talked about their role in advocating and supporting the Civil Union Act (2004), and in doing so summarised the importance of such legislation:

> Judith Collins[3] was on quite early in the piece and she said "so civil unions, it's just gay marriage in another form isn't it?" And I said "no." And she said "well how would you describe it?" And I said "as an option that people don't have now that they really want to have." And she said "oh, so you think people should have things just because they want them, do you?" I said "as a matter of fact I do." And she got really wild at that point. From that point on she kept referring to this as "this amusing submission of yours."
>
> (Tom, 70)

The Marriage (Definition of Marriage) Amendment Act (2013) was another significant piece of legislation that directly impacted the sexual citizenship of the queer community in Aotearoa New Zealand, and one that was brought up in a number of interviews. Isaac described their feelings towards the Act and discussed the value of seeing themselves more included in, and accepted by, society on the basis of their sexual identity. An inclusion that had often been absent for older queer adults prior to marriage equality in 2013:

> I think, in particular, one was very aware of being a second-class citizen. I think a lot of the arguments around marriage equality were to do with becoming a full citizen and having the full range of things that go with citizenship being available to us. And looking back, there was no real likelihood that we would ever really fit in. People would tolerate you, and yes, most people tolerated me and accepted the fact I was gay. And I think I use the word tolerate more than full acceptance. But in those days there was really no sense that gay

people would really ever fully fit in as full members of
society.

(Isaac, 68)

Tom and Isaac were both discussing legislation that was passed
despite facing accusations of granting "special treatment" or
"special rights." Those opposed to civil unions and marriage
equality presented various arguments against them, such as the
establishment of additional benefits and rights for the queer
community, or the weakening of existing social institutions.
Nevertheless, the underlying matter regarding civil unions
and, later on, marriage equality was to ensure that the queer
community had equal sexual citizenship. Sexual citizenship
refers to culturally specific, and often institutionally defined,
forms of belonging that cross the public and private divide of
citizenship. The queer community in Aotearoa New Zealand
has faced extreme regulation, control, and limits in how their
identities and citizenship may be expressed, both in public and
private spaces. The concept of sexual citizenship in this context
exists "at the fateful juncture of private claims to space, self-
determination and pleasure, and public claims to rights, justice
and recognition" (Weeks, 1998, p. 35). The push towards civil
unions and marriage equality were efforts that aimed to achieve
a recalibration of sexual citizenship in Aotearoa New Zealand.
These forms of legislative reform were not specifically related
to forms of stigma, and resulting interpersonal abuse, exclusion,
or attacks, but rather towards discrimination, and the alienation
of the queer community from institutional and cultural markers
of citizenship, belonging, and identity. While these forms of
legislative reform may not remove interpersonal stigma and

abuse – which relies as much on cultural change as legislative and organisation reform – they have begun to challenge normative ideals of sexual citizenship, and as a result, have impacted how older queer adults feel included and able to participate in social spaces.

During the interviews, it became clear that continued advocacy and effort is necessary to improve how older queer adults are able to participate in social settings, particularly in light of the gap between legislative reform and social progress. Despite this, several of the participants noted that younger generations and cohorts within the queer community may perceive the effects of legal changes more clearly. According to the participants, younger members tend to have different expectations and experiences of society as a whole, including their rights as sexual citizens. While the book does not explore this shift in younger queer individuals' attitudes and beliefs, it does highlight how the older generation perceives their community as evolving and growing, which has a direct impact on their access to appropriate social spaces.

Perceived generational shifts

The participants in this book indicated that although legislative shifts may not have changed the minds of those with more entrenched prejudicial attitudes, it may be positively impacting younger members of the queer community and younger individuals in general:

> My suspicion is it's generational. That older women and older guys have a problem, whereas the younger ones are more accepting. And that's not surprising, really, given the changes in general society. I mean for

goodness' sake, up until 1986 it was illegal for me to be in the same bed as another man!

(Jean-Luc, 64)

It is worth noting that the disparity in the perceptions of younger adults could be attributed to a significant shift in the way social connections are established and upheld, not just within the queer community, but also beyond it. The advent of technology and social media platforms has profoundly influenced the way people interact with one another. This digital development has potentially made it easier for young people to express their sexual orientation and gender identity, enabling them to find acceptance and support in a way that was previously unattainable to older members of the queer community. As such, it is reasonable to assume that the changing landscape of social connections has contributed to the differing attitudes of younger generations towards queerness and expectations of social inclusion, in direct contrast to the experiences and reflections of older queer adults:

I think that if you were to talk typically with older people, there would be a lot more stigma and shame. I think that younger people, it's different, and part of that is, I think, social media now. People have access to a lot more information and young people are incredibly computer-literate, and access to YouTube and Tumblr and lots of other things. I think there are conversations that young people have, probably that most older people have not had.

(Rowan, 62)

Rowan's comment above highlights some of the challenges in maintaining social connections and engaging with social spaces for older queer adults – that intergenerational communication and connection can be influenced by patterns of communication that can create boundaries in the wider queer community (Fox, 2007).

When contemplating the potential impact of social policy and legislative changes on the younger members of the queer community, a recurring theme that arose was the significance of fear. Several individuals interviewed for this book expressed the notion that younger members of the queer community experience less apprehension regarding potential negative reactions from society towards their sexual or gender identities. One participant expounded on this topic and linked their personal perception of the evolving nature of "traditional" queer community spaces to this experience of fear:

> There was more a closed society before that. It had to be, obviously. Now, the young ones, who are going out, have no concept of what it was to be frightened to be out in the street and doing all the things that they do. And they go to parties and they take their girlfriends with them, even though they're gay, and the girlfriends bring their boyfriends with them and it's a mess-up. I preferred it if you went to a bar, it was all fellas.
>
> (Benjamin, 76)

It is important to note that queer spaces have constantly evolved and changed over time – with changes reflecting various forms of resistance, community building, and responses to dominant forms of hetero- and cisnormativity (Gorman-Murray, Sullivan, and Baganz, 2022). However, this reflection from Benjamin does highlight how some older queer adults in Aotearoa New Zealand view the younger queer community, with some of the participants – like Benjamin – indicating that these perceived generational changes impact how they engage with queer social spaces. Building on the discussion of social change and development, and the experiences of older queer adults compared to younger queer adults, one participant talked of the difficulty of achieving substantial social change within a generational time frame:

> I look at the whole movement. Racism started to be tackled in the '20s and '30s. It's taken until now for racism … When I was a kid, to call somebody a [racial slur] was perfectly normal. Everybody said it. If I said [racial slur] now, I'd be ostracised from just about everybody. And that's the difference between the 1960s, say, and now. So, it's taken, what, three generations for that. And to be gay we started probably in the '50s. The riots in America started. Stonewall was the beginning of the change. So that means we've got another 20 years to go? There was an article in the paper talking about gay marriage in the States and they said, it's going to go to the Supreme Court, but it's not going to be socially acceptable until the old fogeys die. And that's about what it comes down to: that people my age and older have more conservative upbringing on that issue, and so they have to die off before the younger ones, who do accept it.
>
> (Jean-Luc, 64)

It should be emphasised that the viewpoint put forth by Jean-Luc is just one among various perspectives regarding the shift in generations about the advancement and promotion of human rights. Many older individuals, both within and outside of the queer community, actively advocated for the rights of marginalised groups. Nevertheless, Jean-Luc's perspective highlights an observed trend, albeit stated in more forceful terms, which suggests that despite legislative and social policy reform, genuine transformation of societal and cultural attitudes requires a considerable length of time to materialise.

Legislative change and internal dynamics

The preceding sections of this chapter primarily discussed how legislative changes have influenced the treatment of older queer adults in society, as well as their participation in social spaces. Nevertheless, numerous participants reflected on how social policies have affected the culture within the broader queer community. While I anticipated that the responses to questions about legal changes and developments would centre around human rights, social inclusion, and instances of stigmatisation, these were only some of the frequently discussed themes. Interestingly, some participants highlighted how legislative changes had an impact on attitudes and relationships within the queer community. For example, one participant shared their personal experiences and thoughts on the particular requirements of older queer adults, the issue of ongoing community support, and the challenge of continuing the fight for queer rights:

There's been a significant change of attitude within the community in the sense that in my generation, we were forced to look after one another, because most of the gay community was behind closed doors, and we had to look after each other because the vast majority of society was not going to do that. But now it is different. The doors have opened, the windows have opened. A lot of society has opened its own closet doors. A lot of society itself has come out in different ways and I don't actually believe that law change made a lot of difference. To a degree, it's made life safer for the gay community, but it's also changed an attitude in society in general that there's now "everything's okay … well, you know, you've got your freedom, you've got your human rights" – yeah right – "you've got your civil liberties, so what's the problem now?" The problem is that I think to a degree the gay community is not supporting itself anymore. In one sense it doesn't need to. So, there's an element of neglect. And there are some people who are just falling off the edge because of this social attitude "well everything's all right" – and for some it isn't.

(Liam, 68)

In Chapter 2, we examined the diverse array of strengths, networks, and resources that comprise the social capital connections of older queer adults. These connections provide a supportive and protective environment for these individuals, who often face discrimination and exclusion due to homophobic and heterosexist attitudes and policies. The significance of these social networks is underscored by the concerns expressed by some of the study participants, who fear that a reduction in the perceived need for social capital may lead to a weakening of the networks that support older queer adults.

Conclusion

This chapter has focused on the impact of legislative and social policy changes in Aotearoa New Zealand on older queer adults. The first part of the chapter explored how the participants felt that social policy changes have had little impact on their experiences of discrimination and stigma. Although they noted an improvement in their feelings of safety and security compared to the past, they still believe that discrimination against the queer community remains prevalent. It is difficult to gauge the relationship between legislation and stigma, and perceived generational differences only adds to the complexity of the issue. Ultimately, hetero- and cisnormativity continue to have a negative impact on the social experiences of older queer adults, and their ability to engage with social spaces.

Chapter 1 highlighted that critical social theory challenges the use of law and legislation as a control mechanism (Morley, Macfarlane and Ablett, 2014). This chapter explored how the development of inclusive and protective social policies has impacted older members of the queer community. However, as Liam and other participants in this chapter point out, solely relying on legislation as a measure of social development overlooks the importance of supporting older queer adults both within and outside of the queer community. If social work as a profession accepts this relationship uncritically, it can silence the voices of vulnerable members of the community. Therefore, social workers must remain vigilant and ensure that they do not perpetuate this attitude in their practice.

Furthermore, the views and experiences of the older queer adults interviewed for this book are consistently reinforced by the behaviour and statements of politicians in Aotearoa New Zealand. These actions highlight the discrepancy between legislative reform and social progress. For example, former National Party Prime Minister John Key made a homophobic joke on the radio in 2012, referring to the host's "gay red top" (Stuff, 2012). Former Labour Party Prime Minister Helen Clark was often insulted by being called a lesbian by her political opponents (Stuff, 2009). Health Minister Jonathan Coleman dismissed the notion of publicly funded gender confirmation surgery for transgender individuals as "nutty" in 2015 (Moir, 2015). While National Party Member of Parliament Alfred Ngaro made a speech at a National Party conference in 2017 that many interpreted as homophobic (Wilson, 2017).

Although public figures may not intend to promote discrimination against the queer community, their comments can reinforce stigmatisation (Robinson and Rubin, 2016). Critical gerontology examines the influence of political systems and actions on ageing, including how it intersects with sex, sexuality, and gender. Consequently, politicians' comments and "jokes" require a critical response (Freixas, Luque and Reina, 2012). Additionally, exploring the social capital needs of older queer adults reveals how political structures affect social connections, and can lead to exclusion from social spaces (Oxoby, 2009). From the perspective of older queer adults, homophobic, heteronormative, and cisnormative rhetoric from major political parties in Aotearoa New Zealand reinforces their fears and demonstrates how they are often marginalised from mainstream social spaces.

According to Morley, Macfarlane, and Ablett (2014), social workers possess distinct knowledge, values, skills, and responsibilities to advocate for marginalised individuals whose voices have been silenced or inadequately supported. Therefore, it is imperative to include and listen to the perspectives of those who are impacted by intersectional oppression, especially within the queer community, in critical social discourse.

4
With friends like these

Boundaries, barriers, and the queer unwanted

Learning objective: to identify and analyse the factors that contribute to the complexity of accessing broader queer spaces

After studying this chapter, readers should be able to identify and analyse the various factors, such as sexual orientation and gender identity, that influence the ability of older queer adults to access and navigate broader queer spaces. Readers will gain an understanding of the complexities and challenges faced by older queer adults in their pursuit of social inclusion and support within these spaces.

Learning objective: to evaluate the impact of discrimination and marginalisation on older queer adults within queer spaces

By studying this chapter, readers will develop the ability to evaluate the experiences of older queer adults who have encountered discrimination or marginalisation within queer spaces due to their identities. Readers will explore the effects of these boundaries and barriers on the social inclusion and support experienced by older queer adults.

Introduction

> If you deny any affinity with another person or kind of person, if you declare it to be wholly different from yourself – as men have done to women, and class has done to class, and nation has done to nation – you may hate it, or deify it; but in either case you have denied its spiritual equality, and its human reality. You have made it into a thing, to which the only possible relationship is a power relationship. And thus you have fatally impoverished your own reality.
>
> (Ursula K. Le Guin, 1975)

The relationship between sex, sexual characteristics, and gender has been a commonly debated and discussed topic. Ursula K. Le Guin, a prominent writer in the genre of feminist science fiction, often explored the relationship between gender, sexuality, identity, and community. In a similar vein, this book delves into the social and community ties of older queer adults, touching on related themes. The current chapter focuses on how access to queer community spaces is frequently filtered through the lens of identity. Social spaces are not equally accessible to all members of the queer community due to boundaries and barriers that exist on the basis of sexual and gender identity. To address this issue, it is crucial to acknowledge and comprehend these perceived barriers, which can shed light on the difficulties that some queer community members face when trying to access shared social spaces and networks.

Gay men and lesbian women: "you're you and I'm me"

As a means of investigating the connections between the queer community, social capital, and access to social spaces, several participants shared their accounts of disputes or clashes occurring within queer spaces. These conflicts led to restricted, or reduced, entry to shared social spaces. A commonly expressed sentiment from the interviews was an ongoing animosity between gay men and lesbian women. As Jean-Luc noted:

> Gay men and lesbians. There's an animosity which I'm trying to understand but I haven't yet quite come to terms with it. Partly it's the "you're you and I'm me and ne'er the twain shall meet," and partly it's a lack of our understanding and their understanding. It's just something that happens.
>
> (Jean-Luc, 64)

Jean-Luc attributed the animosity between gay men and lesbian women to a lack of communication or understanding, but it is important to note that this experience may also stem from the privileges that gay men receive due to their patriarchal privilege. The marginalisation and invisibility of lesbian women in queer community spaces could also contribute to this tension. While it was disheartening to hear these narratives of disconnection within queer spaces, it is important to recognise that the early queer spaces and gay liberation movements[4] were formed due to shared experiences of discrimination and stigma. These movements served as a means of solidarity, with the collective goal of creating a more inclusive and accepting society. However, as the queer community grew and diversified, those early relationships began to change:

> In the earlier stages there was a very close relationship between lesbians and gays. But now there's quite a barrier between them, because lesbians – well really it's ridiculous that there should be a close relationship, because men that love men and women that love women – why should there be a close relationship between a gay and a lesbian person? But at that stage it was combined suffering because we were both oppressed on account of the law.
>
> (Andrew, 80)

The significance of examining the connection between gay men and lesbian women is to challenge the perception of homogeneity in queer spaces and settings. Despite ongoing changes within the queer community, perceptions of it by outsiders may remain static. One participant observed that these changes reflect the intricate interplay between social, political, and cultural influences on relationships within the queer community. Specifically, the participant reflected on whether the divide between gay men and lesbian women stemmed from political ideologies or societal attitudes. When asked about her experience of queer spaces, and whether she experienced a divide between gay men and lesbian women, Hannah responded:

> Not as much as there used to be in the '70s when we set up our own lesbian groups, because we didn't want to work with the men then. But that's all a long while ago. There are still pockets of it. I've got friends in Australia. There's pockets of lesbian separatism there and there are pockets in New Zealand of lesbians who want to go on their own stream. What do I think it is? It's more social than political I think.
>
> (Hannah, 72)

Jean-Luc, Andrew, and Hannah's observations are consistent with the existing literature. According to Henrickson and colleagues (2007), both gay men and lesbian women in Aotearoa New Zealand preferred socialising with individuals who share their gender and sexual identity. Insights from the participants in this book suggest that the separation could have resulted from a lack of communication and reluctance to share social spaces, despite experiencing discrimination and having similar political and social goals. In Brickell's (2008) history of gay men in Aotearoa New Zealand it was hypothesised that while initial queer liberation movements depended on the relationship between gay men and lesbian women to succeed – where community solidarity was necessary in the face of extensive public homophobia and bigotry – some lesbian women were eventually turned off by the gay male sexism they encountered in queer spaces. Oral historian Alison Laurie linked this gay male sexism to the increased social acceptance and visibility of the gay liberation movement, which had the result of more conservative gay men joining and lesbian women feeling as if their voices were no longer being heard (Laurie, 2011b). Lesbian women also set up women-only groups, such as Sisters for Homophile Equality,[5] in order to be able to focus on broader issues that also impact women, such as sexual violence, physical assault, and specific healthcare needs (Laurie, 2011b; Willett and Brickell, 2016).

Taylor also looked at this notion of social and cultural separation within queer spaces by arguing that the divide between gay men and lesbian women could be a result of how social environments, or scene spaces,[6] inevitably became dominated by a male presence due to inherent gender inequalities that privileged men's ability to occupy social spaces (Taylor, 2007; 2008). In research that interviewed lesbian women in the United Kingdom about their experiences accessing scene spaces, the participants reported that gay men were afforded more economic power and flexibility, meaning there were more scene spaces available to them and that specifically catered to their needs (Taylor, 2008). Early queer spaces in Aotearoa New Zealand also became segregated by gender due to similar factors, as the spaces available to men were not necessarily available or accommodating of women (Laurie, 2011a; 2011c). Even more formalised early queer organisations in Aotearoa New Zealand, such as the Dorian Society,[7] were not welcoming of women as it was considered as a space for men and men only (Laurie, 2011a). While a lot of these accounts discussed the historical nature of queer social spaces in the gay liberation period, one participant in this book talked about their more recent experiences of queer social spaces being dominated by a male presence. When discussing her experiences of engaging with queer social events, Laura talked about why she was reluctant to attend events that were open to gay men alongside lesbian women:

> That was another reason I didn't go to the dance, it was open to guys too. I do sometimes go to both dances in Nelson, but by the end of the evening, no offence to the guys, they're starting to take out off the shirts and prance themselves and everything else. I find that all too much. That was another reason I decided … When I talked to some of the women about the party, when they left, they said, yes, it was getting to be where the men just take over the whole dance floor. You feel like you're being pushed aside and they're performing and there's like little cockfights and stuff like that. And I just didn't want to have that too. If it have had been totally a women's dance, I might have gone.
>
> (Laura, 65)

As Casey argues "to theorise gay urban spaces as gay male and lesbian … is to forget that both men and women, regardless of their sexual identity, continue to have unequal access to economic and cultural resources and power within public and semi-public spaces" (Casey, 2007, p. 129). These resources inherently privilege access to social spaces, and mean that it is particularly difficult to separate what factors might be influencing the relationships between gay men and lesbian women. Casey (2007) also suggested that several factors such as dependent children, fear of violence, and the limited investment in lesbian women's economic potential have impacted lesbian women's ability to create their own spaces. As suggested earlier (Laurie, 2011b; Willett and Brickell, 2016), these elements could also be factors in the formation of lesbian-only spaces, and this is supported by the statements of the participants in this book. As examined in Chapter 2, many of the lesbian participants talked about their involvement in political and feminist organisations as their early forays into the queer community. As Hannah noted, a lot of these organisations and efforts were focused on the specific needs of women as they intersected with queer experiences:

> With Women's Refuge I was part of the Lesbian Workers and Refuge Group and I did a lot of work there in Wellington. Also, when I worked for Stopping Violence Services, I worked for them for years doing co-gender facilitation programmes, and another woman and I initiated programmes for women with issues of violence and abuse too. It was the first one in the country I think. So that was an extension of my work with Women's Refuge. And because my thinking around and being part of lesbians' communities and what was being provided for lesbians, or bringing up the issues really, because it was not being talked about.
>
> (Hannah, 72)

Hannah's focus, and direction, in her early engagement with queer and feminist spaces was directed by the unequal experiences that members of the queer community face – particularly forms of discrimination and stigma.

The impact of patriarchal privilege is evident not only in the increased presence of gay men in shared queer spaces, but can be seen in research outputs, community initiatives, and the marginalisation of certain members of the queer community who do not conform to mainstream notions of gender and sexuality. Casey (2007) defines this marginalisation as the "queer unwanted," which affects those members of the queer community who are deemed socially, culturally, or economically irrelevant due to factors such as age, disability, gender, and gender nonconformity.

Never mind the "B"

The participants I spoke to drew attention to discrimination that is commonly experienced by bisexual individuals within the queer community. Despite the fact that the acronym LGBTQIA+ includes bisexuality, this sexual identity is often overlooked or dismissed within the broader queer community. As Milly noted, this perception can make bisexual individuals feel compelled to conceal their identity while in queer spaces:

> A friend of mine is bi and she's really positive about it and sometimes, I think why can't I decide one way or the other. Actually in the lesbian community particularly, lesbians can be very negative about bisexual women. I have experienced that. When I've been to lesbian stuff, I've not tended to say I'm bi. I've just pretended I was lesbian. Some lesbians can be totally negative about bi women. So, yeah, I have tended to be cautious around lesbians that I know that are quite political and staunch. Not that I have a lot to do with them, but just, yeah, cautious about sharing that. So yeah, because of that kind of reaction.

> (Milly, 62)

The negative attitude towards non-heterosexual identities may be partly due to the concept of the hetero–homo divide, as some authors have labelled it (Cronin and King, 2010). This binary view of sexual orientation as a scale with heterosexuality on one end and homosexuality on the other reinforces the idea that these two identities are opposites and that individuals must identify with one or the other. This perspective still values proximity to either end of the scale, even though there are various sexual identities that exist beyond these two extremes. The Kinsey scale, a well-known sociological tool used to assess sexual orientation, recognises individuals as existing between 0 and 6, representing exclusive heterosexuality or homosexuality, respectively. However, this scale does not account for identities that exist outside of this binary, such as bisexuality, asexuality, or sexual fluidity. This flaw was inadvertently highlighted during one of the interviews, when Alexander described their own sexual orientation:

> A little sliver of bisexuality in there, but I'm gay. I'm – if you're using a kinseyan thing, I'm 75 per cent gay. I stray occasionally, but I'm gay.
>
> (Alexander, 63)

Even though Alexander used the term bisexuality, it was still expressed from a perspective that viewed bisexuality as a percentage of homosexuality and heterosexuality, rather than as a distinct and separate identity. While another participant, Brain, expressed that his views had changed over time, his belief that bisexuality was a preface to admitting homosexual orientation was somewhat persistent:

> Bisexuals, well my attitude's changed to them over the years. I used to think that they were just queers who wouldn't admit it, and I think some of them still are, but we accept that there are some people who can swing one way or the other now.
>
> (Brian, 65)

Bisexual individuals often face difficulties when accessing wider queer spaces due to the binary perceptions of sexuality that are prevalent in society. These perceptions suggest that people are either gay or straight, ignoring the fluidity and diversity of sexual identities. As pointed out by Erickson-Schroth and Mitchell (2009), this binary attitude towards sexuality can be particularly challenging for bisexual individuals, who may feel misunderstood or invalidated by the limited categories of sexuality that are recognised.

The impact of this attitude towards bisexuality can be significant, affecting not only the mental health and wellbeing of bisexual individuals but also their social inclusion within the larger queer community. Studies have shown that bisexual individuals are at higher risk of mental health issues, including depression and anxiety, compared to their heterosexual and homosexual counterparts (McLean, 2008; Volpp, 2010). Such negative attitudes towards bisexuality can also result in internalised biphobia, causing individuals to feel shame and self-doubt about their sexual identity. This, in turn, can lead to a sense of alienation from the broader queer community. It is essential to recognise that dismissive and hostile attitudes towards bisexuality are not limited to the heterosexual community but are also present within the larger queer community. As Milly reflected, dismissive and hostile attitudes towards bisexuality can result in internalised biphobia, and shows how the perpetuation of the hetero–homo divide negatively impacts bisexual adults in queer spaces:

> But, yeah, I have been negative to myself about it, because it's like sometimes I'll be attracted to a man and I think "oh aren't you done with men yet?" And then I'll be attracted to a woman and, yeah … I can be negative to myself
>
> (Milly, 62)

The presence of binary perceptions of sexuality within the queer community is indicative of the larger issue of heteronormativity in Aotearoa New Zealand. Bisexual erasure has far-reaching effects beyond its impact on individuals who identify as bisexual. Volpp (2010) notes that despite the inclusion of bisexuality in the larger umbrella of the queer spectrum, it is often overlooked and not given separate attention in research related to the mental health of the queer community. In his critique, Volpp points out the shortcomings of such studies that use convenience sampling and fail to differentiate between bisexuality and the experiences of gay men and lesbian women:

> We also need to pay more attention to the intersections of sexual and gender identities to help us answer questions about what might make bisexuals more vulnerable to mental health issues than people who identify as gay and lesbian. By grouping bisexual people in with the gay and lesbian population, we are obscuring potentially important differences involving this sexual minority population.
>
> (Volpp, 2010, p. 48)

This lack of specific consideration in research and community programs that aim to support the wellbeing of the queer community further perpetuates the marginalisation of bisexual individuals – and reinforces binary conceptions of sexuality – ultimately hindering the progress of queer movement towards greater inclusivity and acceptance. It is crucial to acknowledge and address the nuances of different sexual orientations within the community to create a more equitable and supportive society for all, and to create more inclusive social spaces for all members of the queer community.

Bisexuality is just one of many identities within the larger queer community, and unfortunately, the existence of diverse identities has often been met with barriers to accessing queer social spaces. Another group that has faced significant historical and ongoing challenges in accessing these spaces are transgender individuals.

Gender diversity and transgender older adults: "They just don't get trans"

Transgender older adults can face a complex array of social challenges. These challenges are driven by a range of social forces, including but not limited to ageism, transphobia, and cisnormativity. Discrimination and marginalisation based on these factors can be difficult to disentangle, as they often overlap and reinforce one another. As Meyer (2008) observed in research on hate crimes, queer people often struggle to parse out the specific drivers of violence against their gender identity. This is in part due to the social processes that equate gender nonconformity with homosexuality, making it difficult to differentiate between the two.

Related to this, the process of finding appropriate and relatable language, terminology, and labels can be difficult for older transgender adults. The participants who identified as transgender frequently commented on the importance of terminology when referring to their own gender or sexual identity, and how other members of the queer community often met those efforts with hostility. As Jessica commented:

> Sexually, well I'm attracted to women. Definitions are always fraught. If I said lesbian, you can guarantee that there'd be a whole pack of radical lesbians that would attack me for it. I guess I probably am. I'm certainly not interested in relationships with men, so yeah, I guess so.
>
> (Jessica, 60)

During another discussion Bella added a valuable perspective on the issue of hostility towards transgender individuals. Bella highlighted the connection between this hostility and the cisnormative belief that transgender adults are not genuine about their gender identity or are intentionally trying to deceive others. Bella also discussed the link between toxic masculinity and violence towards transgender women, revealing that transgender individuals are often at risk of violence from both within and outside the queer community:

> You'll find with males in particular, and with the activist lesbians, activist lesbians hate us, because they think we're false women. And macho men in particular, if they're of the violent type, their first reaction will be

> anger and then maybe violence. There's quite a high
> murder rate around the world of transsexual[8] people,
> who are doing no harm to them whatsoever – they just
> think that we don't deserve to exist, so they take us out.
>
> (Bella, 68)

The queer community has long suffered from violence, stigma, and discrimination, and unfortunately, these issues are even more prevalent among those who identify as transgender. Research has shown that transgender individuals experience a significantly higher level of discrimination than cisgender individuals (Fredriksen-Goldsen et al., 2011). This discrimination takes a toll on the physical and mental health of transgender older adults, causing physical abuse, psychological distress, and social stigma (Fredriksen-Goldsen et al., 2011; Fredriksen-Goldsen et al., 2014; Levitt and Ippolito, 2014). These negative impacts can be especially harmful to older transgender individuals, who have had to endure a lifetime of societal mistreatment. Moreover, the difficulties that older transgender individuals face in accessing support within the queer community can further exacerbate their struggles. Despite being a part of the queer community for a long time, many transgender older adults still feel like they are not fully accepted or acknowledged. This lack of support and understanding can leave older transgender individuals feeling isolated and alone, compounding the negative effects of discrimination and stigma. Jessica, during our interview, talked about this frustration and concern – and how it often ignored historical connections and trans solidarity with gay liberation movements:

> We interacted a lot with the gay community. We considered ourselves part of the bigger picture. For years we took part in the Gay and Lesbian Fair in Wellington, which turned into Out in the Square and then Out in the Park, and so on. So, we considered ourselves part of that community. Sometimes it got frustrating because there's a lot of people in the gay community that just don't quite get trans.
>
> (Jessica, 60)

Similar to Jessica's account, there have been reports of similar narratives from various sources. International research has found that transgender individuals can experience feelings of exclusion and discrimination within the broader queer community (Fredriksen-Goldsen et al., 2011; Parker, Garcia, and Munoz-Laboy, 2014). One participant, who identified as a cisgender man, mentioned this type of exclusion during a discussion about how the queer community has evolved over time, and the various divisions that have and continue to exist. In this discussion, Andrew talked about the divide between gay men and lesbian women, and touched upon the sometimes contested nature of including queer and gender diverse people in spaces sometimes perceived as existing for gay men and lesbian women:

> So yes there is still a divide. I think it's less of a divide than there used to be, but there's still a divide between men and women. And transsexuals, transgender – they're not gay anyway, or lesbian anyway. Not per se. So they're only with us really because they're queer. They need different considerations, I think, and I'm much less

judgemental about it now. I'm much less judgemental about anybody than I used to be.

(Andrew, 80)

Andrew's comment acknowledges a change in his own views towards the transgender community, but it still implies an attitude of perceiving transgender individuals as separate and not fully part of the queer community. This kind of attitude can create barriers to building social networks and accessing social spaces for transgender individuals, despite the overall inclusivity of the queer community. This can lead to experiences of violence and hostility towards non-conforming gender identities, which are often rooted in processes of homophobia, hetero- and cisnormativity that continue to exist in queer spaces (Meyer, 2008). If transgender adults are restricted from accessing or engaging with supportive social networks within the queer community, they may encounter dual prejudice from the convergence of heteronormative and cisnormative attitudes, putting them at a disadvantage for accessing essential resources and resilience.

"Headspace, willingness, and bravery"

During conversations surrounding queer spaces and diverse identities, one of the topics that arose was the experience of individuals who identify as intersex or gender-fluid. These discussions emphasised the unique challenges that these individuals face, particularly in Aotearoa New Zealand where there is a significant absence of terminology, language, and acknowledgement of these identities. These conversations primarily centred around the experiences of older intersex individuals in Aotearoa New Zealand, highlighting the difficulties they encounter when attempting to express their identity. In this context, Rowan, an individual who identifies as non-binary and intersex, shared their personal journey with me. Rowan spoke candidly about the challenges they faced in coming to terms with their identity and navigating a society that often lacks an understanding of their experiences. Through their story, Rowan highlighted the importance of creating spaces that acknowledge and validate diverse identities, particularly those that are often marginalised or ignored. The discussion emphasised the need to create inclusive environments that recognise and respect the lived experiences of all individuals, regardless of their gender identity:

> I've been queer-identified ever since my late teens, and then this whole process and journey to learn about my intersex reality, which was a fact that was hidden from me as a child, and claiming that and then working out how to hold onto that. So I didn't do that until my forties. So I don't see myself as male or female exclusively, but a wonderful blended combination of both and neither. So absolutely my sexuality as queer, and my gender identity is fluid and non-conforming, and I had to find language for that.
>
> (Rowan, 62)

Rowan's comments shed light on various significant themes and topics surrounding the complex issue of intersex identity. The discussion highlighted a common narrative shared by many individuals globally – the concealment of their intersex identity. As pointed out by Keir and Lahood (2012), this issue is prevalent among intersex persons and can result in long-term emotional and psychological distress. Rowan's personal experience emphasises the challenging and often protracted process of identifying, reclaiming, and acknowledging one's fluid gender identity. Furthermore, Rowan expanded on this journey of embracing their gender identity by discussing the constraints associated with binary gendered language. The societal expectation of fitting into a binary gender construct often limits the vocabulary available for self-expression, which can be frustrating and even invalidating for individuals who do not conform to this system:

> Twenty years ago there was no narrative. There was not even references to other people like myself. It was a profoundly life-changing event to meet other people like myself and to end that extreme isolation that I felt.
>
> (Rowan, 62)

Rowan added to the previous comment by highlighting the importance of community and shared identity. In particular, Rowan reflected on having social connections built on shared experiences, and how that impacted their wellbeing:

> And I think what I would say about that – and I'd say it to you as a social worker and myself as a therapist – we know that community, a sense of belonging is so paramount to good health, and I have a lived experience of that. I don't think we talk about this enough … For quite a long period of doing this work, most of the people that I work with saw themselves within the binary way of looking at things. To step outside

that social construction both required a headspace, a willingness to do that, and an immense amount of bravery. I think most people conform to what society expects them to – it's just intellectually too hard to think about doing something differently.

(Rowan, 62)

While research with intersex and non-binary individuals is limited in Aotearoa New Zealand and much of the world, the research available highlights some challenges that these individuals can encounter when accessing specific social spaces (Behrmann and Ravitsky, 2013; Carpenter, 2016). With some queer community spaces, in particular, being unwelcoming to intersex and non-binary individuals, with little attention paid to their unique needs or desires (Carpenter, 2016). Despite this, in one interview, Liam spoke positively about the efforts of a queer organisation that supports intersex individuals, and how it created an inclusive environment:

I think one of the great joys that I've seen through the development of the [organisation][9] is that diverse groups within the "queer umbrella," if you like, have begun to mix much more. And the Trust itself is so strongly anti-discriminatory in every sense of the word, the expression, because it simply will not close the door on anybody. Of course the focus of the [organisation] is intersex, but it would never exclude anybody because they are primarily gay or primarily lesbian or whatever.

(Liam, 68)

Comments like these highlight the importance of inclusive and welcoming social spaces for all members of the queer community. Accessing safe and supportive communities is vital in the maintenance of social capital and supporting wellbeing for older members of the queer community (Hughes, 2010). However, as long as there are boundaries and barriers in accessing community networks and social spaces for older queer adults, there will continue to be gaps in the support available to this population.

Conclusion

In this chapter we have focused on the various barriers that impede certain members of the queer community from accessing social spaces. By examining the reflections of the participants, we have explored the ways in which individuals with diverse sexual and gender identities interact with each other. This consideration has revealed that there are multiple challenges faced by members of the queer community when attempting to engage in social spaces. These obstacles can range from overt discrimination and prejudice to subtler forms of marginalisation and exclusion. By investigating these issues, we hope to shed light on the complex dynamics and relationships within the queer community. As Liam summarised:

> What I'm saying is, there are boundaries. There are boundaries created within the gay community. And there are signs of those boundaries being pushed away, pushed aside, broken down, knocked down – whatever expression you want to use – but they're still there for a lot of people. They are there – those walls.
>
> (Liam, 68)

The major theme throughout this chapter has been that relationships and connections in the queer community are still filtered through social constructions of identity. As a result of these social categories, not all members of the queer community have been afforded the same ability to access social spaces. For older adults in the queer community that can mean that potential support networks and social connections are not universally available. The purpose behind this chapter was not to present an overtly critical view of the concept of queer community, but rather to challenge assumptions that all individuals who identify under the LGBTQIA+ acronym are the same, and to draw attention to the need for strategies that can support the entire queer community.

As previously discussed, several participants noted an animosity between gay men and lesbian women. This observation can be linked to a few different factors. For instance, prior research has explored the concept of scene spaces and how gay men are often granted greater access as a result of their economic flexibility. Additionally, some scholars have suggested that a range of societal influences contribute to the greater difficulty that lesbian women experience in attending social gatherings. It is evident that lesbian women face the negative effects of patriarchal privilege and invisibility, which not only impedes their ability to participate in queer scene spaces but also undermines their inclusion in exploratory research and community initiatives.

Similarly, the narrow perspective that sexuality can only be classified as either gay or straight disregards the existence of bisexuality, both in the larger society and within the queer community itself. This chapter reveals that bisexual erasure is not limited to a lack of recognition, but also encompasses adverse opinions and beliefs leading to internalised biphobia. The participants conveyed that the queer community can be just as inflexible in its stance on sexuality as conventional heteronormative societies, potentially ostracising certain individuals.

Additionally, during the discussions about perceptions towards transgender and gender diverse individuals in the queer community, a recurrent theme emerged. The participants expressed that they felt their identities were not recognised by other members of the community or were sometimes met with hostility. To challenge binary perceptions about gender, one participant pointed out that it takes a combination of headspace, willingness, and bravery. Nevertheless, the work to achieve this goal is still in progress within the queer community.

The overarching thread of these findings is that the relationship between identity, access to social spaces, privilege, and oppression is complex. It can be hard to separate and define what influences individual and community relationships. However, despite this challenge, it is evident that the wider societal views about sexuality, gender, and gender express can be equally present in the queer community.

5

Adding silver to the rainbow

Age, ageism, and queer spaces

Learning objective: to understand the impact of age and age-based discrimination on individuals within the queer community

By studying this chapter, readers will gain an understanding of the specific challenges faced by older queer adults due to ageism. They will explore the ways in which ageism affects their ability to access social spaces, form intergenerational connections, and receive support. Readers will develop insights into the unique experiences and needs of older queer adults within the broader queer community.

Learning objective: to analyse and address the prevalence of ageism within the queer community

Readers will examine the concept of the "queer unwanted" introduced in the previous chapter and its extension to older queer adults. They will critically analyse the factors contributing to ageism within the queer community and explore its implications. Through this objective, readers will develop strategies to address and challenge ageism, promoting inclusivity and support for older queer adults within various social environments and intergenerational contexts.

Introduction

> If you are pining for youth, I think it produces a stereotypical old man, because you only live in memory, you live in a place that doesn't exist … I think ageing is an extraordinary process whereby you become the person you always should have been.
>
> (David Bowie, 1999)

The quote by David Bowie above highlights a common reflection that emerged during the interviews – the participants' contemplation of how age and ageing had transformed them. While the experiences were not always positive, ageing was a journey of introspection and personal growth. Throughout this journey of reflection, the participants in this book have consistently emphasised the significance of social spaces. These spaces played a crucial role in facilitating the development of social capital, supporting political movements, and fostering various social relationships within the wider queer community. This chapter focuses on the concerns raised by the participants in relation to accessing social spaces. In particular, it notes that the participants felt they were no longer included due to their age.

The findings reported in the chapters 2, 3, and 4 have all pointed to the need for carving out social spaces for older queer adults. In this chapter we explore the impact of age and ageism on older queer adults. By addressing general perceptions on ageing, the chapter examines how a youth-centric culture and the invisibility of ageing sexuality hinders how older queer adults access social spaces. The reflections and experiences of the participants discussed in this chapter highlight a growing concern for social work practice and policy: How do we support older members of the queer community considering age-based exclusion, discrimination, and fear?

The participants I talked to all shared one common characteristic: they were classified as "older adults." Despite the socially constructed and subjective nature of ageing, all of them are considered as older adults by most standards of social science literature (Settersten and Hagestad, 2015). As each participant was aged between 60 and 80 at the time of their interview, the components of ageing and ageism intersected with our discussions on social capital, queer social spaces, and wellbeing – and were not solely focused on experiences within the queer community. Jessica, when touching upon the subject, noted that general presence of ageism across society:

> There is an emphasis on youth. It's probably a societal thing, not just the gay and lesbian community, but the "life's a party" sort of mindset. I think they tend to look down their noses a little bit at the older generations,

which is a shame because there's stuff that they could learn, I think.

(Jessica, 60)

In line with Jessica's observations, Brian echoed a similar perspective, noting that an emphasis on youth and the "life's a party" mentality is not unique to the queer community. He opined that it is just the nature of being young – seeking out people who are similar to oneself. Brian's remark suggests that ageism is a pervasive issue in our society, rather than being specific to the queer community:

I just think it's in the nature of being young. You're just looking for people like yourself, and I think probably that young straights are much the same as well. So older people don't really exist for them.

(Brian, 65)

Not all of the participant's comments on ageing were solely centred on the attitudes of others, as some reflected on their internal perceptions and thoughts about getting older. These reflections highlighted the complexity and multidimensionality of ageing and ageism. One common theme that emerged was the internalised stigma related to ageism. Several participants discussed feeling shame or a sense of failure at the prospect of getting older. They revealed that the cultural narrative around ageing is often one of decline, and that this narrative had affected their self-perception:

I have insecurities like every other human being – like getting older. You're not the pretty young thing anymore and all that kind of stuff and there's all those insecurities, but those don't have a thing to do with your sexuality. That's just around ageing and all those other issues that everybody in the world deals with.

(Alexander, 63)

The effects of internalised ageism can be particularly challenging for older adults within the queer community. As with other forms of internalised oppression, internalised ageism can intersect with internalised homophobia, leading to further stress and anxiety for older queer individuals (Van Wagenen, Driskell, and Bradford, 2013). This compounded effect highlights the importance of considering the unique experiences of older queer adults in discussions of ageism. Furthermore, some of the participants noted that ageism might be more prevalent within queer spaces than in general social settings. This observation adds another layer of complexity to the experiences of older queer adults, as it suggests that they may face additional barriers to social inclusion within the queer community.

Ageism and dismissal – "go home grandad!"

Ageism refers to the negative stereotypes and attitudes towards older adults that lead to their devaluation and exclusion from participating positively in society (Kane, 2004). In this section we explore the impact of ageism on the participants in this book. Acknowledging that ageism and other social forces frequently overlap, it's essential to note that certain interviews emphasised generalised experiences of ageism that may not be explicitly tied to the specific experiences of older queer adults. For example,

Fiona acknowledged that her experiences of ageism were influenced by her gender:

> You can say it's paranoia, I suppose, but there's just sometimes in some situations less consideration, I think, for the older woman's opinion. I think our society is still geared for the young and I think it's still male-dominated a lot.
>
> (Fiona, 73)

In Chapter 4, we discussed how the intersections of identity within the queer community lead to the allocation of diverse social privileges and disadvantages among its members. It was pointed out in that chapter that due to patriarchal privilege, gay men are more likely to access and occupy social spaces compared to other members. Similarly, the impact of ageism is also gendered. Anna emphasised the societal pressure on women to conform to conventional beauty standards, which often include looking youthful. Such societal expectations and norms disproportionately affect women, and as a result, they may face additional barriers in social spaces as they age:

> I think ageism is built into our society, so that for women what is promoted is the youthful and the beautiful, and that the old and the wrinkled are rather beyond the pale.
>
> (Anna, 75)

Anna's comment illustrates the intricate interplay between ageism, gender, and sexuality. For women, ageing is often linked to a loss of visibility and a lack of acknowledgement by society at large (Lemish and Muhlbauer, 2012). When this is combined with the marginalisation and prejudice faced by the queer community, it poses even greater challenges to the wellbeing of older lesbian, bisexual, and transgender women.

The pervasiveness of ageism in the lives of the participants was highlighted independent of their demographic background or intersectionality with other social stigmas. The participants recounted numerous occasions when they felt their opinions and experiences were discounted solely because of their age. Such patronising and dismissive attitudes towards older adults ignore their ability to contribute meaningfully and share valuable life experiences. Jean-Luc shared his frustrations regarding the prevalence of this attitude:

> As you get older, "oh you old fuddy-duddy," "oh you don't know anything." "You don't know what's happening," whereas in fact it's the reverse. I've been there, done that. I have seen what's happened and I continue to see what's happening and the problem belongs to you, not to me.
>
> (Jean-Luc, 64)

Tom also talked to this process, and the impact this had on him while engaging with public spaces:

> I have noticed that people sometimes don't take me as seriously as they used to. And I think that's got something to do with being older. People think that if you're old you must be soft in the head. People have a stereotype of older people too. I'm aware of that. I don't think I look quite as old as I am and so that probably gets me over that hump a bit. But now and again

somebody will refer to me in the third person as being old and it always comes as a bit of a surprise and shock to me. I was in a bar one afternoon, talking to one of the bar staff that I know, and there was a guy down the bar with his girlfriend and he must have been listening in to our conversation. And something I said made him laugh and his girlfriend must have said, what are you laughing at, and he said "I'm laughing at something the old guy said." So you run across that. You suddenly see yourself as others see you.

(Tom, 70)

Mark built on this narrative and shared his experiences of pervasive, day-to-day ageism, particularly related to negative comments in public spaces. He recounted several instances where he felt disrespected and devalued due to his age. For example, he talked about being ignored or talked over by younger people in public places, and how this made him feel invisible and unimportant:

One that really bugs me the most was probably about five years ago, walking down Courtenay Place here on a Friday night – or a Saturday – not too late, round about 9 or half-past 9 or something like that. And there were a couple of young kids – young kids to me – probably 17, 18, or something like that – sitting on the pavement. One of them yells out to me "Go home grandad, it's time you were in bed." You know, that sort of thing – ageism, and it's often.

(Mark, 75)

The social construct of ageism is characterised by attitudes, beliefs, and practices that perpetuate negative stereotypes about ageing (Gendon et al., 2015). These stereotypes often lead to patronising or condescending behaviour towards older adults. During the interviews, Anna was asked whether she had experienced any changes in the way people treated her as she aged. Anna responded by sharing her experience of having her neighbours and friends assume that she needed constant assistance. Although the behaviour was not overtly negative, Anna felt that it highlighted an assumption of her inability to take care of herself simply because of her age:

> Neighbours come and offer to do things for you, because you're old, and you don't really want … I mean you don't not appreciate the fact that they're offering to help you, but you don't really want it. You're still capable yourself. It's so current in this society.
>
> (Anna, 75)

In addition to comments that dismiss and marginalise older adults in society, ageism is also prevalent in the workplace. As supported by previous research (Brooke and Taylor, 2005; Davey and Cornwell, 2007), older adults are often overlooked and discriminated against in terms of employment opportunities. This trend of ageism often commences with comments that suggest older adults should retire and exit the workforce once they reach a certain age:

> I think it's a little bit of, hmm, "Aren't you retired? Didn't you want to retire? Why don't you stay retired?"
>
> (Liam, 68)

The subtle ageist attitudes can negatively impact the career trajectories of older adults who wish to continue working, leading to discrimination in job interviews, promotions, and other professional opportunities. Moreover, such practices perpetuate the false stereotype that older adults are less productive, less capable, and less valuable to society. Another challenge faced by older adults is in entering the workforce after a period of not working, or having left a previous role. As Jessica reflected, she had a suspicion that her job applications were turned down on the basis of her age:

> One thing I have noticed, and it's not related to being transgender or anything, it's just age, period. When I handed in my notice at work I applied for a number of jobs and the job market is difficult. I applied for a few jobs that I thought were within my capabilities and what have you, but I never even heard anything. My suspicion is that they look at your age and you just get put into the discard pile automatically. When you're pushing 60 it's a whole different ball game. It was interesting, I was listening to Michèle A'Court, she's a comedian and actress and writer and stuff, on the radio yesterday and she was saying that the roles on either stage or screen that she used to do, she doesn't get offered them anymore. It's age, and it's a reality that you just have to accept to a degree. But it makes life a hell of a lot more difficult.
>
> (Jessica, 60)

During the interviews, another participant shared a disheartening experience when she moved to Aotearoa New Zealand from

Australia. She was repeatedly exposed to dismissive attitudes and was denied employment opportunities, which ultimately led her to believe that she was no longer able to seek future work based on her age. This participant's experience illustrates the challenges that older adults face in seeking employment opportunities, especially in a new country where they may not have established social networks or support systems:

> Even coming back since then, I had four job interviews when I came back, cos I was on leave without pay with no guarantee of work when I came back. I had four job interviews, was unsuccessful. They are jobs that I could have done really easily and really well. Every job they employed somebody a lot younger than me – and to the extent that I have decided I'm never ever gonna apply for another job, go through an interview process, if you know what I mean. I'm past my use-by date.
>
> (Natalie, 65)

Employment provides various benefits to support the wellbeing of older adults. In addition to providing financial stability, it also offers access to social spaces and networks, which can be crucial for social engagement, a sense of purpose, and accomplishment in later life (Fredriksen-Goldsen et al., 2015; Seligman, 2011). However, as highlighted by the interviews in this book, ageism can restrict their access to these benefits by limiting their opportunities to secure employment. The impact of ageism is not limited to attitudes and comments from others but can also lead to exclusion from social institutions and spaces. For instance, as Jessica noted, she suspected that her job applications were rejected based on her age.

Gay people are never gonna get old

Older adults with diverse sexual and gender identities face ageism in various aspects of their lives, but the participants in this study often expressed concerns regarding the restrictive attitudes towards age in the queer community. The participants identified two distinct issues: a pervasive emphasis on youth in queer spaces and the belief that sexual identity loses relevance as one ages. The interviews included specific questions about the impact of age and ageism in the queer community, such as whether or not the participants felt discriminated against in queer social spaces. This focus was intended to gain a better understanding of the ways in which ageism impacts older queer adults access to social spaces, including queer-specific spaces, and how this affects their overall wellbeing. Moreover, it aimed to explore how these experiences of ageism intersect with other aspects of identity, including sexual and gender identities. As such I inquired whether or not the participants had felt a sense of ageism in queer social spaces:

> Oh huge. That may be a bit of overstatement. Well it's a very youth-oriented … Look at the media; look at any of your gay publications and all that kind of stuff. Everybody's young and they look like a model and you're not gonna see a lot of older people in those, because "gay people are never gonna get old." Somehow, they think that.
>
> (Alexander, 63)

In this statement, Alexander pointed out one of the most significant themes that came out of the interviews, which was the feeling of exclusion experienced by many older members of the queer community. According to Alexander, a common attitude expressed by younger individuals, and even some queer spaces, was that older people did not belong in queer social spaces. This type of exclusionary mindset is prevalent in society, and it can be hurtful and isolating for older members of the community. Despite the presence of queer community groups and networks designed explicitly for older adults, many older queer adults still encountered dismissive attitudes, which made them feel unwelcome in queer social spaces. As a result, they found it challenging to connect with others and build supportive relationships, leading to a lack of social capital and feelings of loneliness and social isolation.

Building on this topic, some participants discussed the generational divide within the queer community and how it affects their social interactions. According to Jean-Luc, younger members of the queer community tend to frequent nightclubs and similar locations, while older adults prefer other types of social spaces. This divide can lead to a lack of contact between generations:

> Yes, well that's an unfortunate reality that younger people tend to socialise in nightclubs and so on. Older people tend to have done that, been there, and no longer are interested.
>
> (Jean-Luc, 64)

Jean-Luc's comment about older members not wanting or being willing to socialise in nightclubs and similar venues is further explored later in this chapter. However, the notion that differences in preferred social spaces solely divide different generations within the queer community was not a consensus view among other participants. Benjamin argued that older members faced hostility when attending shared social venues with younger queer adults:

> It can be vocal as well. I've been at the sauna and elderly chaps come in and try to make contact with somebody. They say "fuck off, you old bastard," that sort of thing.
>
> (Benjamin, 76)

However, it was not just spaces designed for socialisation where older queer adults encountered ageism, but also in spaces and organisations that were designed to promote the wellbeing and inclusion of the queer community:

> It can crop up. When I was on the board of [organisation],[10] we always had a stall Out in the Square and you could hear it occasionally amongst the younger generation. There would sometimes be an age tension about "well that was then when you were all living in the closet," "this is a young person's party, why don't you oldies just go away. You had your time."
>
> (Liam, 68)

Related to this experience, a common issue that emerged during the interviews was the impact of age-related stereotypes in the queer community. Sean spoke about this issue and highlighted that it is not just limited to a specific location but is a global problem. Sean emphasised that ageism is a pervasive issue in the queer community, which is exemplified by the popular belief that individuals over the age of 30 are no longer relevant or desirable:

> It's something that gay people around the world talk about, and the old "if you're over 30, you're in a different category" sort of thing.
>
> (Sean, 69)

The effects of ageism and age-related stigma on older members of the queer community are undeniable. However, it is not only the blatant forms of ageism that the participants reported. Another common experience of ageism within the wider queer community was the feeling of being invisible or unnoticed. Despite being present, some participants felt that they were not worth acknowledging or considered as part of the community by younger adults. This experience of being overlooked or dismissed because of their age left them feeling isolated and disconnected from the community:

> I'm just invisible there. No one's unkind or anything, but just invisible. You walk through the door and everybody's young. I'm not upset by that. It's kinda silly. You could have a much better time if you had a whole range of people, but that's the case. Yes it's a very youth-oriented kind of culture.
>
> (Alexander, 63)

Brian talked about similar experiences which matched with Alexander's narrative:

> I just think that the pretty young things don't even see us. We're just not there. Because they're only looking for people like themselves.
>
> (Brian, 65)

According to previous research, older members of the queer community often face barriers when trying to establish successful intergenerational communication, as age is frequently considered a hindrance to forming such relationships (Fox, 2007). Such hindrances can be seen as yet another example of social structures that negatively impact the wellbeing of older adults, and this is a matter of great concern for older queer adults. This is because social spaces for the queer community are already rare, and age-based exclusion only exacerbates the difficulty in finding such spaces (Casey, 2007; Chambers, 2004; Kim, Lehning, and Sacco, 2016). A critical gerontological perspective highlights the importance of addressing age-based exclusion in social spaces and the need for intergenerational connection to be fostered in the queer community. This is essential for the wellbeing of all community members, regardless of their age or other intersecting identities.

Exploring how ageism operates and is facilitated in the queer community is a complex process. While it is easy to point to stereotypes of older adults, the invisibility associated with age, and instances of direct abuse, ageism also operates in more subtle ways. One of these other types of insidious ageism comes in the form of recognising sexuality. In particular, the notion that one of the participants described as "once you get old you cease to be gay." Part of the challenge for older members of the queer community is that society generally views older adults as nonsexual beings (Chandler et al., 2004). This perspective does not recognise the sexual history, experiences, and ongoing impact sexuality has on the identity of older adults. As such, older adults generally lose an aspect of their identity, and older queer adults can find themselves not acknowledged in broader discussions around and within the queer community. As Samantha summarised:

> Nobody thinks about your sexuality if you're an older person, older woman – there's just the assumption. You have to make a very definite statement to people that you're a lesbian if you want that to be known at all.
>
> (Samantha, 72)

Beth also described the lack of acknowledgement about her sexuality:

> That's another thing about getting older: you don't get asked anything that has anything to do with sexuality. Oh dear, it just never comes up.
>
> (Beth, 65)

The significance of sexual identity for a person's overall sense of self cannot be understated (Hughes and Heycox, 2010). Not acknowledging the sexuality of older queer adults can have severe repercussions on their wellbeing and identity, particularly as sexuality was a defining part of many of these individuals' identities during times of activism and social change. Moreover, many people in the queer community were unable to marry their same-sex partners or have a civil union because of legal restrictions. Therefore, symbols such as Mr and Mrs titles or wedding rings may not be present to signify a sexual relationship.

To promote the wellbeing of older queer adults and their access to social spaces, all facets of their identity, including their sexual orientation, must be recognised and supported. Failing to do so would exclude these individuals from the broader queer community and, by extension, society at large. Fiona eloquently addressed the importance of this topic as she reflected on the relationship between age, sexuality, and identity:

> Across the board, older people can lose their sexual identity. It can be seen by younger people that they mightn't have any interest or any ability to feel sexual. I've read books, not necessarily about lesbians or gays, but I have read some of them in the older age group and they do have a sexual identity still and they may want to explore that. They may want to be in a sexual relationship. So if you're not in an environment that's comfortable and safe, then you put all of that down and then the person you were, you're already losing a whole lot of parts of yourself because of your ageing, and then you lose another part as well.
>
> (Fiona, 73)

Ageism remains a significant challenge for older queer adults, limiting their access to wider queer social spaces. This prejudice can manifest as queer spaces being geared towards younger people or the false notion that sexual identity is no longer relevant for older adults. Consequently, older queer adults face more significant obstacles in accessing the same level of social opportunities as their younger counterparts.

Conclusion

Ageism is a pervasive issue that affects a significant number of older adults. Ageism can take many forms, including how older adults are perceived and treated by others, but it can also lead to internalised ageism. This can cause older adults to question their own self-worth and value in society, perpetuating the continued dismissal of their contributions. While ageism affects many older adults, the participants in this book also highlighted ageism that was specific to the queer community.

The participants expressed frustration with the youth-centric culture present in many queer spaces, leading to a feeling of being excluded and overlooked. This ageism is compounded by the assumption that sexual identity is not a concern for older adults, further removing a critical aspect of their identity. Notably, not all of the comments made by the participants focused on external perceptions of ageing. Many reflected on their own internal perceptions of getting older and the stigma that they had internalised. This internalised stigma is a critical aspect of the ageing process, often leading to a questioning of one's self-worth and value in society.

6

Towards equality in care

Understanding the needs of older queer adults in healthcare and social services

Learning objective: to identify the challenges faced by older queer adults in healthcare, social services, and aged care

After studying this chapter, readers will be able to recognise and articulate the unique challenges that older queer adults encounter when accessing healthcare, social services, and aged care. They will gain an understanding of discriminatory attitudes, ignorance, and lack of understanding that can negatively impact the wellbeing of this population.

Learning objective: to analyse the intersection of ageing and the experiences of older queer adults in social spaces

By engaging with this chapter, readers will develop the ability to analyse how ageing intersects with the experiences of being an older queer adult and the specific concerns that arise. They will explore the realities of relying on social spaces to support the ageing process and gain insights into the implications of this intersection for the wellbeing and support needs of older queer adults.

Introduction

> The doctor in this small town said "well, you're not going to carry on with these practices here, are you?" I think that sort of influenced me to say "well, actually I really do want to have a gay doctor."
>
> (Mark, 75)

In this chapter, we will explore how older queer adults engage with healthcare professionals, social services, and aged care as they navigate the ageing process. Mark's experience highlights the importance of understanding the attitudes and knowledge of helping professionals towards the queer community, as well as the significance of creating inclusive and supportive care environments for older queer adults.

Previously in this book, we examined how shifts in legislation and social policy have impacted the daily experiences of older queer adults. Building on this, we will now focus on how the attitudes and knowledge of helping professionals towards the queer community can affect the wellbeing of older queer adults seeking supportive services. As a broad term, helping professionals encompass social workers, counsellors, psychologists, general medical professionals, and aged care providers.

In this chapter, we will explore how older queer adults seek out supportive care and services, including their preferences for queer-identifying practitioners and the impact of dismissive or discriminatory attitudes on their wellbeing. Specifically, we will examine the intersection of ageing and queerness, as well as the particular concerns and challenges faced by older queer adults in accessing healthcare and social services. We will also explore how aged care services can be tailored to meet the needs of older queer adults, including the importance of respectful and reflexive practice among healthcare professionals and aged care providers. Through this exploration, we aim to highlight the importance of creating inclusive and supportive care environments for all historically marginalised populations.

Engaging with professionals

As I talked to the participants in this book about their experiences of engaging with social spaces, and in particular about engaging with healthcare and social services, a consistent experience that was relayed to me was about the discrimination they faced in these particular contexts. As a result, the participants recounted their hesitancy to disclose their sexual or gender identity to professionals, and found it easier to do so only when they felt safe, secure, and had built up a trusting relationship with the other person. This hesitancy is complicated by the fact that, in some circumstances, disclosure is required before trust can be built, such as when engaging with healthcare and social services. Research has shown that members of the queer community are less likely to seek help and support services due to the fear of identity-based discrimination (Croghan, Moone, and Olson, 2014; Neville and Henrickson 2010). This is especially true for helping professionals such as doctors and medical practitioners. In response to this fear, the participants reported actively seeking out professionals who were part of the queer community. Mark aptly summarised the importance of this decision:

> Well, I've chosen always, while I've lived in Wellington, to go to a gay doctor. And the reason for that is that being gay, sex is part of your life, and discussing aspects of your sexual behaviour, one needs to be comfortable about. And I've always felt more comfortable talking to a gay man than I would to a straight doctor.
>
> (Mark, 75)

Mark then went on to explain that this idea of feeling more comfortable with a gay doctor came from early experiences and interactions with medical professionals:

> I think probably my first experience talking to a doctor about sexuality was when I was a teenager and I was getting concerned about being gay. It wasn't called "gay" in those days – it was "homosexual" and some other bad words. And I went to the family doctor, because I was concerned about how I was feeling, and he said "Oh, don't get mixed up with those guys – they'll never let you go." That was the sum total of his advice. As it turned out though, in subsequent years I realised that I was pretty lucky, because in those days a

different sort of doctor would say "Okay, well we need to change you," and you would have been engaged in other things which today we recognise as being very harmful. So I guess that response was better than some responses I could have had. And he didn't tell my parents, which was important to me. Yeah, so, I think that experience probably influenced me.

(Mark, 75)

These narratives are consistent with previous research, which highlights the pervasive discrimination that older queer adults face in healthcare settings. A study by Fredriksen-Goldsen and colleagues (2011) found that 13 per cent of older queer adults reported being denied healthcare or receiving inferior care because of their sexual and gender identity, and up to 20 per cent did not disclose their identity due to fear of discrimination. In this book, the participants shared how their early experiences with medical professionals were not always explicitly discriminatory. For instance, Jean-Luc suspected that their psychiatrist held homophobic beliefs, but lacked the language and self-awareness to confirm their suspicion.

When I was 17 or 18, the very first psychiatrist, I wasn't quite aware of it myself, so I didn't really know, but the sort of questions he was asking was a bit homophobic. But I didn't really understand myself, so I couldn't challenge it.

(Jean-Luc, 64)

Expanding on the idea that overtly offensive behaviour was not always the primary concern, many participants in this study highlighted the significance of their queer identity being dismissed by professionals. While overtly homophobic comments and attitudes were noted, the more pervasive issue was the lack of recognition and importance given to their sexual and gender identity.

Dismissive attitudes

During the interviews, the participants did not always describe the attitudes and actions of helping professionals as overtly homophobic. Instead, they commonly discussed the dismissive nature of practitioners towards their sexual or gender identity. Such attitudes may reflect heteronormative and cisnormative values, which fail to recognise the importance of sexual and gender diversity (Willis et al., 2016). This is concerning, given the historical experiences of queer adults who have faced stigma, discrimination, and abuse throughout their lives (Brennan-Ing et al., 2014), as similarly reported on in earlier chapters. For practitioners who work towards promoting wellbeing, psychological distress, or day-to-day health, it is crucial to consider all influencing factors. Sexual and gender identity and related experiences are central components of the wellbeing of older members of the queer community. It was this reason that Alison emphasised when they discussed the need to change doctors when the doctors were not mindful of the impact of sexual identity.

> I've had doctors who, yeah, definitely I've had to change because they've been very much ... just dismissive of it more than anything, I think. Like not seeing it as an important part of me, of who I am. That it's not something that they want to put into the conversation

– where my doctor now, very much it would be part of the conversation, where some it's like "oh no, that's not important" where actually your lifestyle and who you are is important to whatever you're talking to your doctor about. So yeah, I've had that in the past.

(Alison, 60)

Alison expressed that one of the advantages of getting older was feeling more comfortable and empowered to express the importance of finding professionals who were accepting of her sexual identity. Inquiring further, I asked Alison if she had ever experienced any discomfort or hesitancy when disclosing her sexuality to professionals with whom she interacted:

That's probably because I picked my doctor, for that to work. Like I know, you get to a doctor and you see how that goes, and you change if it doesn't – again that comes with age. Realistically, as I've got older, I want whoever I have as a doctor to be someone that I'm comfortable with, and she's fantastic. Counsellor – same thing. I made sure it was a counsellor that was very good with that, and they either had to be okay or, if it wasn't, I was going somewhere else. So again, it comes with age, being able to do that. Where again, someone younger, you go to a counsellor, are you going to have the balls to say "actually no, this doesn't work"? It's hard, that sort of stuff – where I will, now that I'm older.

(Alison, 60)

The comfort level of older queer adults in accessing services is not solely influenced by the attitudes of helping professionals. The extent of knowledge regarding specific needs also played a crucial role in how participants perceived the quality o care and support they received.

Lack of knowledge

The interviews conducted revealed the prevalent issue of healthcare practitioners lacking knowledge about the specific needs and experiences of the queer community. This was particularly evident for the transgender older adults I talked to, which is similar to findings reported in global literature (Siverskog, 2014). The lack of knowledge extended to areas such as before and after gender confirmation surgery, the significance of hormone treatments, and the importance of addressing patients by their preferred gender identity. For instance, a participant mentioned being assigned to a male ward despite identifying as female during her hospitalisation.

> I've been up in the hospital. I think I've had a bit of discrimination up there. I've noticed that they put me in a male ward instead of a female one.
>
> (Katheryn, 78)

A lack of professional knowledge for working alongside transgender individuals is not a new finding, as previous research has shown a dearth of trained workers in this field (Veldorale-Griffin, 2014). This was evidenced in the experiences of the older queer adults I talked to, as Bella told me about their interactions with psychiatrists, and subsequently needing to seek private services as a result of this lack of knowledge:

Bella: What I found is ... when I had something to do with [name of service[11]] people, they don't know anything about transgender people.

David: So there's a lack of knowledge there?

Bella: It's quite sad. You've got to go out to ... My therapist was a private company. Those connected with the crisis teams and the hospital groups don't seem to know about us and they don't know how to deal with us. That's my personal experience.

(Bella, 68)

Despite evidence of a general lack of knowledge about diverse sexual and gender identities among health professionals reported in international literature (Sharek et al., 2015), many of the participants reported positive experiences with well-trained and open-minded professionals. While there are issues with a lack of training and knowledge, it is also equally important to highlight the experiences of those who have had positive encounters with healthcare providers who are accepting and knowledgeable of their unique needs.

Competent professionals

One of the more affirming themes in the interviews was the positive experiences that people had with supportive helping professionals who acknowledged and validated their diverse sexual or gender identity. For instance, a participant who was reflecting on their experience of transitioning stated:

When I first started my transition, I had a doctor who was in the gay community, and he was the best doctor for those that were transitioning. He knew exactly what was going on. I think it was easier, because, when I talked about things he knew actually what I was talking about.

(Katheryn, 78)

Similarly, when I asked Jessica about potential discrimination from professionals, they responded:

No, hell no! No, John was really good because he had worked in Australia and he had done a lot of work – I think he told me he'd worked with about 700 trans people, so he had a really good understanding of that situation. Yeah, he was excellent. He was excellent. It was funny, just about every time I had an interview with him he had one of his students there, so there was a student there every time, so it was quite an educational thing for the students. Because from what I understand there's virtually nothing taught about trans stuff in med school.

(Jessica, 60)

A recurring theme in these discussions was the lack of training and education for medical professionals on diverse sexual and gender identities. Jessica's comment highlights this concern, which was echoed in many of the interviews. As previously discussed, research has shown that social work education often overlooks the needs of queer people and fails to challenge heteronormative views of students (Rowntree, 2014; Logie, Bridge and Bridge, 2007). The impact of this gap in education was highlighted when Rowan shared their experiences working in the queer community, and how they had encountered practitioners who lacked the necessary knowledge and skills to work with queer clients:

> The other part of it is actually challenging the professionals who work with us, to become more skilled, challenging transphobia, homophobia – the sorts of things that make it difficult for people to be healthy and well. There's not enough people that do this work, and there's certainly not enough people who are GLBTI-friendly in New Zealand.
>
> (Rowan, 62)

As Rowan had extensive experience in providing therapy to the queer community, I asked whether they had observed any changes in the attitudes of helping professionals over time. Specifically, I was interested in whether there had been a generational or cultural shift in their knowledge and competencies. When I broached the topic, Rowan shared their thoughts on how things might have evolved in the past two decades:

> Ooh, that's a good question. I think that there is a lot of people out there who are genuinely respectful, warm, intelligent people, but this issue is not covered in most of our training still. I'm involved in a wonderful new programme at the Auckland Medical School: It's an elective paper for fourth-year medical students that was developed last year, and it's being taught this year and we now know it's going to be taught again next year. That's the first time in the history of medical training in New Zealand that this issue has been addressed.

Expanding on this, Rowan clarified that lack of knowledge is not necessarily due to the discriminatory attitudes of professionals, but the fact that there is a lack of specific queer content in training and education in Aotearoa New Zealand:

> So when we say that professionals in this field are not very skilled, it's not because they don't want to be – it's because the issue hasn't been addressed. Now, I work very closely with an organisation in Australia called the GLBT Health Alliance, and the research that's coming out of Australia is that our community, our rainbow community, is somewhere between 12 and 15 per cent of the general population. So if you think 12 per cent, 15 per cent of the population is not being well looked after by the caring professions – and I'll sort of open that up to doctors, mental health workers, social workers, everybody – yeah, we're talking about a huge number of people.

(Rowan, 62)

Rowan raises a crucial point that highlights the potential harm caused by a lack of specific training for helping professionals. If practitioners are not equipped with the necessary knowledge and skills to work effectively with diverse sexual and gender identities, then a significant portion of the population may not receive the appropriate care and support they require. This could result in many queer adults feeling marginalised and discriminated against, leading to further issues related to mental health and wellbeing.

The perception of hostility: homophobia and cisnormativity on planning for aged care needs

Care anticipated ... more accurately care dreaded.

(Willis, et al., 2016)

The quote above, from a study in Wales that explored what older queer adults expect from care providers, touches on a central theme of this book: That for older queer adults the prospect of relying on, or engaging with, aged care services is actively dreaded. This dread begins with the concerns of older adults generally in relation to a loss of independence, lack of autonomy, and a fear of isolation, but is compounded further by specific fears that relate to queer identities and experiences. During the interviews we talked about how the participants witnessed social and cultural changes. While these conversations began as broad topics, allowing for the participants to explore their own ideas in the context of the research, universally the discussion moved to a particular topic – planning for the future. Building on these topics, this half of the chapter examines the relationship between ageism, heteronormativity, and cisnormativity; the specific fears that older queer adults had about entering this stage of their lives; and the role small communities have in meeting the needs of older queer adults they age.

Ageism and heteronormativity

The relationship between ageism and hetero- and cisnormativity was often described by the participants as manifesting in the form of language and attitudes. In one interview, Beth, who worked in a rest home at the time of the interview, had reflections on how ageist and heteronormative language infiltrated the culture of aged care facilities. These reflections from her work included broader concerns than just fears relating to sexual and gender identity. More precisely, she focused on how staff would talk about residents and how gossip infiltrated these environments. Beth was initially asked if she had much experience with residents who were out about their sexuality, and it developed into her speculation about the impact of staff behaviour on limiting opportunities for residents to be open about non-heterosexual identities:

Beth: This is my third facility I've worked in, and being gay as a resident – well I've never spoken to anybody who has said "I'm a little bit ….""I've just never met anybody. Everybody has identified as being heterosexual.

David: Do you think that's a fear of coming out or just a coincidence?

Beth: It's probably both. I think that probably I would avoid coming into a place like this with [name of partner]. I know how these girls talk about the residents behind their backs. So I would probably avoid it, at all costs, coming into a facility like this with her.

(Beth, 65)

Following on, Beth talked about how the lack of private spaces and a patronising attitude contributed to her aversion to entering a rest home. It was not just about expression of a queer identity or being in a queer relationship, but rather the fact that any expression of intimacy from older adults was treated as an "adorable, cute action," or as a novelty factor for staff – as opposed to a valid and central part of an older person's life. This is a frequently reported concern for older adults and is a manifestation of patronising ageist attitudes that strip older adults of their autonomy and personhood (Chandler et al., 2004). This "elder talk," or the language of ageism (Gendon et al., 2015), exists both overtly and covertly. It is why the fears of older queer adults are not just related to queer experiences – they are inherently tied to the broader social construction of ageism. Yet despite the general fears associated with age, ageing, and attitudes towards older adults, the interviews provided examples of specific fears related to queer sexual and gender identities.

Specific fears for older queer adults

An obvious question that arises when considering the fears and needs of older queer adults is how they differ from those of older adults generally. Previous research has found that older queer adults experience homophobia in rest homes (Fronek, 2012; Johnson et al., 2005), and identity-based discrimination also limits socialisation opportunities in residential care settings (Brennan-Ing et al., 2014; Chandler et al., 2004). As Liam explained, their fear about going into care ranged from having to re-enter the closet, losing socialisation opportunities due to their queer identity, to broader losses of independence:

> It's something that I increasingly think about – not quite on a daily schedule, but pretty frequently. My former neighbour here at No.2 is in [*retirement village*][12] just along the road here and I go and see him fairly

frequently. And my immediate reaction, as nice as it is, David, and as well-kept as it is – God forbid that I end up in a place like this. Because as a gay person I don't think I would fit in here. I really don't. I would probably stay in my little apartment and never come out again, except to see like-minded friends, and that scares me. It's a hard one to answer really, other than to say yes, I do have deep concerns about growing old and what quality of life I will have, especially if I do grow old on my own.

(Liam, 68)

Mark had a similar perspective, and talked about an example of when they visited a friend in rest home, and the concerns that raised for him:

A friend that I used to sail with a lot, he ended up in his last couple of years in a rest home as well. And I used to go and see him twice a week – I did this religiously. We'd been friends for a long, long time and I'd made it my mission to make sure that he had plenty of encounters with the outside world. And his behaviour in the home was very much keeping it secret, because he didn't feel safe there to be openly gay. And it's not so much the staff, but it's the other inmates, if you want to call them that. They've been brought up – of that age – brought up where homosexuality is really bad, and if you're gay or if you're a homosexual, you're a bad person. If he had come out in that environment, then those people could have become very hostile. And so his life amongst the other people could have been very unhappy, and so he chose to keep his sexuality to himself. To me that was sad. Obviously I had to respect it. And that really made me start thinking that actually there is an issue here – that it doesn't matter how much the rest home itself tries to be safe for gay people, it relies very much on other people who are living there as older people accepting gayness as being okay.

(Mark, 75)

An interesting comment Mark made above is that this fear is not tied to entering a rest home specifically, but that it was dependent on the behaviour and views of the residents themselves. This is why a common thread in the interviews was about the need and desire for specific queer retirement and rest home facilities.

"Wouldn't it be nice?": queer facilities and services

Many of the participants experienced abuse and discrimination from their peers throughout their lifetime. They expected that older adults of their generation would still be carrying those same biases and attitudes that negatively impacted them, which is why they were often selective in choosing their community and social spaces. While the participants often chose, or tried to choose, queer-friendly communities and networks to associate with, it can become more difficult when entering a rest home or relying on care providers. As a result of these reflections, some of the participants considered whether specific queer-based rest homes and retirement options were better suited to their needs and experiences:

Every dinner party of older queers gets to talk about this at some stage. It's always along the lines of "wouldn't it be nice if we could buy a block of flats together and have one flat for a carer, that they could live in rent-free, and we'd all chip in to buy" – that sort of thing. Just recently a lesbian retirement home project has just fallen over here in Auckland. I don't know how far it got, but it's just fallen over. I was involved in a housing co-op many years ago, and we paid some money into it for a feasibility study and it didn't get off the ground in the end. The property, which was in Ponsonby/Freemans Bay, was sold to a developer who developed units on it, much the same as we would have put on. There's a Jewish old folks' home and there's a Dutch old folks' home in Auckland, and I quite like the idea of there being a queers old folks' home, but I don't think it's going to happen.

(Brian, 65)

This same desire emerged when I was talking with Jean-Luc:

Yeah, one of the big issues, we've had a group set up to look at gay retirement places – I won't call them villages – but somewhere where gay people can go and not be anonymous. Because a standard residential rest home, there is a certain amount of discrimination, and what I've heard is that gay men suddenly are hidden again. Their orientation is not allowed – and that's wrong. A gay man should be allowed to have a man in his room. That will change over time. As I say, 30 years in the future it won't be an issue, but right now with older people mixing with other older people who have dissimilar attitudes, you'll have discrimination.

(Jean-Luc, 64)

One interesting topic brought up in these discussions about rest homes and specific queer needs was who these facilities might cater for. As discussed in Chapter 4, historical and contemporary divisions within the wider queer community have been a point of contention for some of the participants. Specifically, for gay men and lesbian women there have been arguments about general versus specific spaces for queer adults. These same arguments were carried over into the interviews about creating queer-friendly rest homes:

> Well, it would be nice to be around other lesbians, gays or alternatives, in a communal setting but I don't know that the population's big enough to sustain it really. And I don't know, see it's interesting, because there's always been that separatism. So I see the lesbian elders going off as a separatist kind of movement – when I think I was always part of that too in my younger days, wanting that for lesbians and lesbians only and all that stuff. But I don't know now whether it's better to be working towards integrating so we can get some services within the broader framework and I think probably that's the way to go, because of the population.
>
> (Hannah, 72)

Similar to the point made by Hannah about working together on behalf of the whole queer community, Brian highlighted the important distinction between a rest home for gay men and a gay-friendly rest home:

> No, I wouldn't want it to be just gay men. But it would
> need to be a gay-friendly place. Yeah, it would need to
> be gay-friendly.
>
> (Brian, 65)

Brian explained that gay-friendly, in this context, referred to an environment where sexually diverse individuals could be open about their identity without facing consequences from staff and other residents. Facilitating the development of queer-friendly environments requires that care staff are trained in working with and respecting diverse identities, that the physical environment promotes positive queer spaces, and that stigma and discrimination within facilities is not tolerated. On this topic of training and knowledge for aged care staff, in some of the interviews, participants discussed their specific concerns about a lack of knowledge and training to support gender diverse and non-binary older adults.

Gender diversity in aged care

As the interviews for this book were conducted with a broad range of participants, including people who identified as transgender, intersex, or gender-fluid, discussions on the potentially unique challenges for gender diverse older adults in aged care were brought up:

> I'm on my own basically for everything, so I have no
> idea. I'd just have to keep looking after myself as long
> as I possibly can. I understand where they're coming
> from because the systems that are in place for looking
> after elderly people have no conception about trans
> people or gay people. Well, they have a little bit more

understanding of gay and lesbian people I think, but trans people is just way off their horizon. And I can only deal with my own situation, which is probably not dealing with it at all, simply because I don't have the resources to deal with it. But there are other trans people that will have the resources and they're gonna have to face it and, to be honest, it's something that the society as a whole has to learn to deal with. This sort of work is important to make those changes happen because otherwise nobody's ever going to change anything. But it's a tall order. It's a tall order.

(Jessica, 60)

Jessica went on to talk about the fact that for transgender older adults in residential care there would be no one-size-fits-all approach to working with and supporting those older adults. Jessica described why this would be the case, as well as talking about her own desire to be involved in training and upskilling residential care staff:

Trans people, there's differences within the community as well, with individuals, because there are post-operative or pre-operative or non-operative people. And when you're dealing with an elderly person, those are things that you're gonna have to be aware of. You're not just dealing with somebody that's in one body or the other; sometimes there are both there. So they need to be aware of it. If I had the energy at the moment, I would be quite happy to talk to people in the staff situation so they had a better understanding of it, but right at this point – well, I'd be happy to go down somewhere and talk to somebody. I don't have the energy to organise it. If somebody said "There's a group here that needs talking to; can you come and do it?" Yes, I'd do it, no problem. But it's just the organisation that's off-putting. But, yeah, it needs to happen. It needs to happen. Over the last couple of years I've heard talk of things happening within the gay and lesbian community but not in our community. And we're going to be the trickier one for them to deal with.

(Jessica, 60)

In another interview, Rowan talked about the work they were currently doing in supporting a transgender woman who had recently entered residential care, and in doing so described their observations:

I'm supporting at the moment a transgender woman that I've worked with for a number of years who's just recently gone into an aged care facility. And these things have been on my mind somewhat because I'm observing both her experiences of going into this facility and just watching how people are treated in there, and it horrifies me. We should be looking after and treasuring our old people and valuing them, and I'm not sure that we're doing that as a society. I know we do that individually with some families, but as a selective society I think we've got some huge work to do there to improve the situation.

(Rowan, 62)

Conclusion

This chapter looked at the complicated relationship between legislative changes and social development on the professional skills, competencies, and prejudices of helping professionals. Some participants selectively engaged with practitioners with a queer background due to previous negative encounters with professionals. Participants were concerned about the discriminatory or dismissive behaviour of helping professionals, but also noted a lack of knowledge and training contributed to a lack of inclusive services. These concerns were not limited to sexual or gender identity but also intersected with ageist attitudes. The overlap of heteronormativity and ageism can cause older queer adults to be hesitant to seek supportive services, leaving a significant portion of the population unsupported.

Emerging out of discussions about the impact of dismissive or unknowledgeable practitioners, the interviews in this research all touched upon a common concern of the participants – how they would be treated by aged care services. Primarily, it was not the fear of how staff would treat them, but how other residents in aged care services would react to their identity. The participants in this research believed that older heterosexual and cisgender adults would carry the same biases as they had experienced throughout their lifetime. As a result of these beliefs, the participants were actively fearful of entering residential care. As such, the participants frequently discussed with peers the possible benefits of specific queer facilities, or the need to provide upskilling and training to staff and facility managers.

7

Breaking barriers

Social work models for empowering older queer adults in social spaces

Learning objective: to understand the multilevel approach of supporting older queer adults within social spaces

By studying this chapter, readers will gain knowledge and comprehension of the micro, meso, and macro levels of social work and social services in relation to supporting older queer adults. They will be able to explain how these different levels intersect and contribute to the overall wellbeing and inclusivity of this population within social environments.

Learning objective: to analyse and apply conceptual and practical models for supporting older queer adults

After engaging with this chapter, readers will be able to compare and contrast the conceptual model and the paradigm for practice presented within the text. They will develop the ability to evaluate the structural forces that impact older queer adults and understand how these models can inform and enhance social work practice. Readers will be able to apply these models in real-life scenarios to better support and advocate for the needs of older queer adults within social spaces.

Introduction

> We should indeed keep calm in the face of difference, and live our lives in a state of inclusion and wonder at the diversity of humanity.
>
> (George Takei)

This quote by George Takei captures the essence of the key messages conveyed throughout this book: the critical role of inclusion and diversity in social spaces. As social workers, it should be our collective ambition to advocate for the inclusion of older queer adults through practice, policy, and research. The stories and experiences shared by the group of older queer adults interviewed in this book serve as powerful tools to aid in this advocacy effort, bringing to light the lived experiences of this demographic.

In the previous chapters of this book, I have presented the central findings of my research. Here, in the final discussion chapter, I want to link the key components of those chapters, and answer the research question initially presented in Chapter 1 of "how do older queer adults navigate space, community, and social environments?". Drawing on the findings of this research, I have presented a conceptual model and a paradigm for practice designed to inform social work practice at micro, meso, and macro levels. These models translate the findings of this research, and the narratives presented in this book, in order to support older queer adults.

The intersection of wellbeing, social spaces, and older queer adults is a topic of significance not only to myself but also to the social work profession in Aotearoa New Zealand. The ageing population of Aotearoa New Zealand is expected to access social services in unprecedented numbers by 2046, including those provided by social workers (Abendstern et al., 2012; Statistics New Zealand, 2013; SuperSeniors, 2016). As a result, social work practitioners need to be equipped with sufficient knowledge, experience, and culturally sensitive practice to effectively engage with this growing cohort (Bergh and Crisp, 2004). Moreover, with the increasing numbers of older queer adults accessing social services in tandem with the general ageing population (Fredriksen-Goldsen and Muraco, 2010), it is crucial for social workers to be cognisant of their unique needs stemming from their historical and contemporary experiences with heteronormativity and cisnormativity. The insights gleaned from the experiences of older queer adults in this book, which are briefly summarised below, underscore the importance of developing social work practice and policy that is best suited to support this population.

The political–social dynamic of social spaces

A frequently reproduced sentiment in this book is that older queer adults occupy a distinctive social perspective, in that they have lived through significant periods of legislative and social policy changes regarding sexual and gender diversity (Van Wagenen, Driskell, and Bradford, 2013). As a result, it was important to me to explore how changes in Aotearoa New Zealand legislation impacted the social capital and access to social spaces for the participants in this book.

The interviews I conducted revealed that the social capital networks of older queer adults function differently compared to those of their heterosexual and cisgender counterparts. Their experiences of living through historic events have greatly influenced the nature of their social connections, as well as the types of resources that are valued within them. The participants emphasised the importance of close and supportive relationships, particularly in times of personal distress, which formed as a result of having lived in a time where homosexuality was illegal and socially unacceptable. This led to the formation of tight-knit communities that provided mutual support. The interviews also highlighted the significance of reciprocity and trust in the development and maintenance of positive social relationships among older queer adults.

However, the impact of legislative and social policy changes, and their perceived value by older queer adults was debated. A significant number of the participants acknowledged that legislative changes did little to curb social stigma, and even protection under anti-discrimination laws did not change the day-to-day experiences of this community. That is not to say the participants did not reflect on the impact of broader social changes over the last few decades. A few noted that general societal attitudes towards queer adults have tended to improve, even if experiences of abuse, discrimination within social services, or public derision of diverse sexual and gender identities were still unfortunately frequent.

The largest impact of the legislative changes in Aotearoa New Zealand for older queer adults has been on regarding the concepts of identity and citizenship. One participant noted that the arguments for civil unions, and eventually marriage equality, were founded on the idea of being equal citizens – being able to enjoy the same cultural rights and participate in the same activities as heterosexual individuals. These developments have been important in how the participants saw themselves as being able to take part in Aotearoa New Zealand society and access social spaces.

Identity and inclusion within the queer community

One of the main questions within this book involves a sweeping, overarching generalisation. Specifically, the query "what is the connection between social capital and wellbeing for older queer adults?" poses a risk of assuming homogeneity and disregarding the diverse identities and experiences that make up the term "queer adults." This inclination to presume uniform characteristics within the queer community is widespread in the social sciences and other social discourses (Cronin and King, 2010). Consequently, it was crucial for me to investigate: How do various members of the queer community encounter and engage with social spaces?

The stories and accounts presented in this book shed light on the intricate dynamics of relationships and connections within the queer community. These interactions are heavily influenced by societal constructs of identity that favour certain individuals over others, particularly in terms of sexuality, gender identity, and age. Consequently, specific segments of the queer community enjoy greater visibility, consideration, and influence due to historical and contemporary notions about who belongs in queer spaces. One of the central discussions revolves around the division between gay men and lesbian women. Many participants reflected on how patriarchal privilege continues to grant men, irrespective of their sexual orientation, economic, cultural, and social advantages that enable them to shape and occupy social spheres. For instance, social events often tend to be male-dominated, and early political movements in Aotearoa New Zealand advocating for the decriminalisation of homosexuality became less inclusive towards lesbian involvement (Laurie, 2011a). It's worth noting that both lesbian women and some of the queer men who took part in this research acknowledged this divide. However, the male participants were less inclined to acknowledge their own male privilege, instead focusing on the historic legality of same-sex activity between women versus men. The lack of awareness among the participants regarding the experiences of other members of the queer community complicates the examination of how people share and interpret shared social spaces. This lack of understanding can create barriers for older queer adults in both establishing and embracing social networks, which ultimately detrimentally affects the wellbeing of individuals and communities alike.

Identities within the queer community can mirror the binary constructs ingrained in broader social structures. It's important to recognise that even though certain individuals in the queer community may reject binary perspectives of sexuality, gender, or gender identity, binary viewpoints still exist within queer spaces. Consequently, the stigma and dismissal stemming from these perspectives can significantly impact individuals within queer social environments. For instance, binary notions of sexuality that perceive it as a linear spectrum between gay and straight risk diminishing the validity and legitimacy of bisexual identities. In my research, I observed similar attitudes, with bisexual individuals feeling excluded or facing judgment due to their sexual orientation. Binary systems also influence perceptions of gender, where cisnormative beliefs that strictly divide people into male and female categories often disregard the experiences of transgender, intersex, and non-binary individuals. The participants in this study shared similar experiences within the queer community, leading to feelings of exclusion, isolation, and sometimes even hostility.

Lastly, ageism emerged as a shared experience among the participants in this study, further highlighting another dimension of identity that imposed barriers within many queer social spaces. This unfortunate reality disregards personal preferences, individual needs, and practical considerations, particularly affecting older queer adults. As a consequence, these broad queer social spaces may not adequately cater to their unique requirements or backgrounds, thereby limiting their options for accessing vital social support.

In addressing this particular question, I have explored the intersection between identity, access to social spaces, privilege, and oppression. Articulating and evaluating the impact of these relationships on social capital and wellbeing is complex, but necessary in order to advocate against social work services and practices responding with a one-size-fits-all approach for members of the queer community.

Aged care and aged concerns

The process of preparing for the potential reliance on aged care services or transitioning into a residential care facility is one that many older adults encounter (Yeung et al., 2017). Although not all older adults require such services, expressing apprehensions regarding this transition is prevalent among them (Sharek et al., 2015). In the case of older queer adults, these concerns revolve around fears of losing independence and autonomy, as well as anxieties stemming from their unique experiences as queer individuals.

The participants featured in this book faced a distressing intersection at the prospect of aged care services, where their encounters with ageism converged with the stigmatisation resulting from heteronormativity and cisnormativity. These individuals believed that they would confront a double jeopardy, as these services were unlikely to cater to their specific needs as queer adults while simultaneously lacking the consideration typically afforded to older adults (Duffy and Healy, 2011). As discussed in earlier chapters, legislative changes do not automatically translate into shifts in social attitudes or the competency of professional service providers. Consequently, it can be inferred that residential care facilities and general age-based services will inherently harbour individual and professional biases against diverse queer adults. Although all the participants in this book were residing independently within the community at the time of the interviews, their expressions of fear reflect the concerns held by older queer adults about their engagement with social spaces as they age.

Social capital and social spaces

Throughout the chapters of this book, my aim has been to dissect various aspects of a broader inquiry: investigating the role of social spaces in the wellbeing of older queer adults, and evaluating the practical relevance of the social capital model within social work practices involving this demographic.

Previous research has suggested that social capital plays a crucial role in enhancing wellbeing by granting access to a wide range of resources (Talo, Mannarini, and Rochira, 2014; Wilson, 2006). These resources include aspects like social participation, fulfilment, community engagement, and a sense of solidarity (Talo, Mannarini, and Rochira, 2014; Theurer and Wister, 2010). Social capital serves as a model for evaluating the presence of valuable resources, interpersonal and community resilience, and the overall quality of relationships and networks (Oxoby, 2009). The findings from this book indicate that social capital holds significance for older queer adults, as it fosters connections between individuals, establishes trust and reciprocity, and facilitates the exchange of valuable resources, all of which contribute positively to their self-perceived wellbeing.

In addition to presenting narratives, experiences, and insights into diverse communities and interpersonal relationships, this book aims to go further. It strives to illustrate the potential impact of applying a social capital-informed practice model on the wellbeing of older individuals in the queer community. To achieve this, we need to delve into the connection between social justice, structural systems, and social work in Aotearoa New Zealand. By understanding these relationships, we can develop a practice model that encompasses micro, meso, and macro components.

Social justice, structural systems, and social work

Social work should embody the principles of social justice (MacKinnon, 2009). Social justice involves pursuing political, social, and cultural goals that prioritise diversity, meeting basic needs, fairness, and equality in treatment and outcomes (Craig, 2002). This framework is inherently intertwined with social work practice, aligning with the definition of social work by the International Federation of Social Workers, as well as the principles and code of conduct supported by organisations like the Aotearoa New Zealand Association of Social Workers and the Social Workers Registration Board (ANZASW, 2015; IFSW, 2023; SWRB, 2023). In essence, this means that social work, whether it involves direct practice, advocacy and policy work, or the education of students and practitioners, is driven by the objectives of fostering social cohesion, empowerment, and liberation for all individuals (Brown, 2006; Fook, 2002; Forrest and Kearns, 2001; Nygvist et al., 2013).

These perspectives and goals are fundamental principles in applying critical social theory and critical gerontology (Fook, 2002; Freeman and Vasconcelos, 2010). As discussed in Chapter 1, the aim of this book is to take the narratives and stories of older queer adults and align them with the objectives put forth by critical social theorists. These objectives include individual and community liberation, addressing hidden forms of social control, and promoting personal freedom (Guess, 1981). For social workers supporting older queer adults, working towards these goals requires considering their historical experiences and present concerns. This process also acknowledges that these past experiences continue to impact the wellbeing, community connections, and sense of belonging for older queer adults in present-day Aotearoa New Zealand. Recognising hidden forms of social control requires social workers to examine how the portrayal of queer adults in media and the comments made by influential figures contribute to their marginalisation. Chapter 3 presents some examples of this control for discussion, although they represent only a fraction of the daily stigma faced by older queer adults. Finally, promoting personal freedom involves incorporating the feedback and suggestions of older queer adults into all levels of social work services while actively critiquing and challenging the influences of heteronormativity, cisnormativity, and ageism in broader society and within the field of social work itself.

Social justice and the profession of social work

The social work profession aims to promote both social justice and human wellbeing. In this book, I pursued these goals by giving prominence to the concerns of older queer adults in Aotearoa New Zealand and considering the implications of the findings. Keenan, Limone, and Sandoval (2016) argue that social justice and wellbeing should be seen as a unifying purpose, and their study identified three themes relevant to supporting older queer adults.

The first theme is the need to challenge injustice at all levels of practice, including micro, meso, and macro interventions. The second theme highlights the importance of constructing justice through relationship and resource organising, which can be supported by the social capital model. The final theme emphasises the creation of accepting environments within service providers and wider social contexts.

While social workers often recognise social justice on a micro level in their day-to-day practice, incorporating it on meso and macro levels requires more time, collective action, and may be less immediately apparent. These findings have implications for supporting older queer adults, suggesting that efforts to promote their wellbeing and social justice must be incorporated across all levels of practice. This includes addressing biases in services and policies, advocating for inclusive policies within larger government systems, and recognising the complexity and scope of practice models that incorporate social justice principles.

Power systems in social work

These findings highlight the importance of addressing social justice at different levels of social work practice, from micro to meso and macro levels. It is crucial for social workers to recognise and challenge power systems such as heteronormativity, cisnormativity, and ageism that affect older queer adults. Legislative changes alone may not significantly impact the daily experiences of this community, emphasising the need for critical reflection within the social work profession. The profession should move beyond measuring progress solely through legislation and engage in internal critique to avoid inadvertently reproducing power systems. Advocacy and critical engagement with marginalised communities should be complemented by self-reflection within the profession. The social justice component of social work is seen to be weakening, with an emphasis on individual identity and neoliberal policies (O'Brien, 2011). Models of practice should incorporate advocacy for macro level change, while the profession must be mindful of its role and influence within power structures.

Research conducted in Aotearoa New Zealand suggests that social justice principles should be incorporated at multiple levels of social work practice. A study found that social justice is relevant at the micro, meso, and macro levels (O'Brien, 2011). Micro level practice involves addressing immediate needs of individuals and families within systems that may not adequately support them. Meso level practice requires challenging organisational policies and practices that perpetuate marginalisation. Macro level practice involves advocacy, lobbying for change, and collective action from professional bodies (O'Brien, 2011). For older queer adults, these dimensions of practice are influenced by specific considerations, and the social capital model provides a framework for identifying and working within these dimensions (Barker and Thomson, 2015; Baum and Ziersch, 2003; Healy and Hampshire, 2002; Mental Health Commission, 2009).

In the following discussion, the findings of this book, combined with the theoretical framework, are presented in the form of a conceptual model that outlines some of the structural forces impacting older queer adults.

Micro, meso, and macro: practice, policy, and pedagogy

The model below (Figure 7.1) shows the dynamic interactions between the structural forces impacting older members of the queer community, the impact these can have on the ability of this population to access social spaces, as well as how internal relationships can both support and hinder older queer adults.

For older queer adults, cisnormativity, heteronormativity, and ageism all influence how they can participate in society and access social spaces. These social structures impact their citizenship and political autonomy, it informs the competency and attitudes of professionals who work with this population, and perpetuates stigma and discrimination.

Citizenship and political autonomy

In Figure 7.1, the concept of citizenship pertains to the rights and privileges that older queer adults should have access to, on a par with heterosexual and cisgender individuals (Ewikj, 2009). This encompasses their entitlement to human, social, and cultural

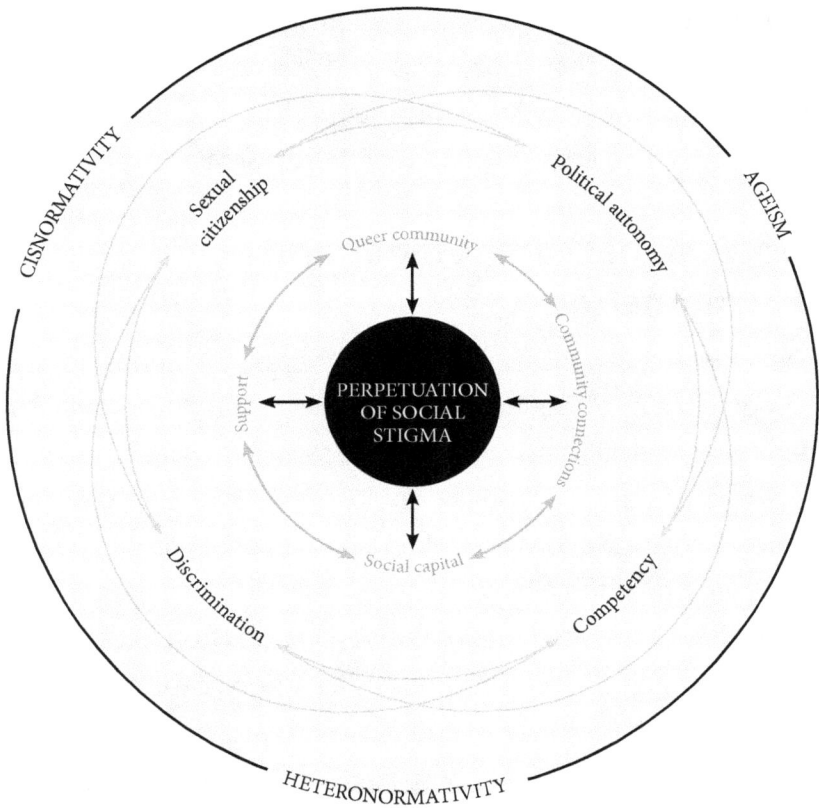

Figure 7.1 Political and social influences on older queer adults

rights, such as education, employment, and social protection. While legislative and social policy advancements have granted older queer adults greater social and cultural rights, citizenship also encompasses their ability to engage in society without fear of abuse, recognition of their sexual and gender identities by government entities, and equal levels of visibility. Political autonomy encompasses similar aspects, but also involves the capacity of older queer adults to influence political systems and receive respect from those systems. The older queer adults whose stories and experiences are highlighted in this book were keenly aware of how heteronormativity, cisnormativity, and ageism affected their citizenship and political autonomy. The field of social work must provide support to this population to help them attain equality in both of these domains.

Professional competency and discrimination

The influence of these structural forces also extends to the competence of professionals and social services. Cisnormativity, heteronormativity, and ageism collectively devalue the lived experiences of older queer adults, and it is possible that educational institutions for helping professionals, as well as the agencies where they work, can perpetuate these biases. In this book, I have presented accounts and narratives from older queer adults that corroborate this finding, as a significant number of participants shared their encounters with professional services that were hostile and demonstrated a lack of knowledge and skills in working with this population.

Furthermore, these forces have a direct impact on discrimination. In Aotearoa New Zealand, older queer adults face discrimination in both obvious and subtle ways. The participants in this research frequently reported experiences of discrimination, which persisted throughout their lives. While verbal abuse appeared more prevalent than physical threats as they aged, the continuous effects of discrimination on their wellbeing and sense of safety are evident.

The queer community: supportive relationships and internal dynamics

As depicted in Figure 7.1, the queer community possesses mechanisms for supporting and safeguarding itself against these structural forces. Interpersonal connections, the presence of social capital, and mutual support serve as avenues for developing resilience to these forces while also providing a foundation for challenging them. The narratives in this book underscore the significance of interpersonal relationships, community, and the exchange of emotional support as vital components for maintaining wellbeing. Social capital was employed to highlight the distinct processes underlying these forms of support, shedding light on the unique aspects of the social networks to which older queer adults belong.

The impact of these structural forces also influences the internal dynamics of the queer community. The participants in this study expressed the challenge of navigating multiple identities, especially when encountering negative attitudes towards those identities. Instances of this within the queer community include historical tensions between gay men and lesbian women, dismissive views towards bisexuality, and disregard for gender diverse individuals. Age emerged as another common factor influencing relationships among the participants. Ageism was a prevalent experience for older queer adults in this study, affecting their relationships both within and outside the broader queer community. These attitudes and behaviours can further strain the fabric of the queer community and limit the support networks available to individuals who are already marginalised by wider social structures. This has led to the emergence of a subgroup sometimes referred to as the "queer unwanted" (Casey, 2007). It is essential to continually engage in critical analysis, recognising that the multiplicity of identities, access to social spaces, and the interplay between privilege and oppression are intricate and nuanced.

Purpose of the conceptual model

The aim of Figure 7.1 within the context of social work, is to underscore the profound impact of broader social structures. By doing so, it establishes a foundation from which to challenge and critically examine these structures. The imperative of critical social theory and critical gerontology, which necessitates recognising social forces that adversely affect vulnerable individuals before they can be confronted (Dant, 2003), compels practitioners and researchers to acknowledge the diverse identities present within communities. Building upon this recognition, the next step involves translating these insights into practice.

Drawing on the principles of social justice, particularly within the social work profession, I have been able to develop a practice paradigm based on the narratives within this book, informed by the model of social capital. This paradigm incorporates the conceptualisation of social capital, encompassing bonding, bridging, and linking capital, while integrating the research findings. It serves to highlight areas of micro, meso, and macro level practice that can be developed to provide support for older queer adults, aligning with principles of social justice.

Paradigm for practice with older queer adults

Figure 7.2 introduces a practice paradigm that draws upon the insights uncovered in this book. In constructing this paradigm, I incorporated the theoretical framework of critical social theory and critical gerontology. Furthermore, I employed the model of social capital to underscore the significance of nurturing supportive and distinct relationships within the queer community. Ultimately, the objective of this paradigm is to align with the principles of social justice and inform practice accordingly.

As mentioned earlier, social justice serves as a guiding framework that informs various aspects of social work practice, research, and education. Its principles form the foundation for practice at international, national, and local levels (Keenan, Limone, and Sandoval, 2016). Social justice encompasses universal aspirations that are relevant across all dimensions of social work; nevertheless, the specific application of these aspirations varies depending on the context. Figure 7.2illustrates how, for older queer adults, the areas of practice can be categorised into micro, meso, and macro layers.

Micro

Within the micro dimensions of practice, the focus lies on working directly with individuals and families to address their immediate needs (O'Brien, 2011). For older queer adults, these needs arise from their experiences as a minority population in a society that often overlooks their specific requirements and fails to recognise the discrimination they face on interpersonal

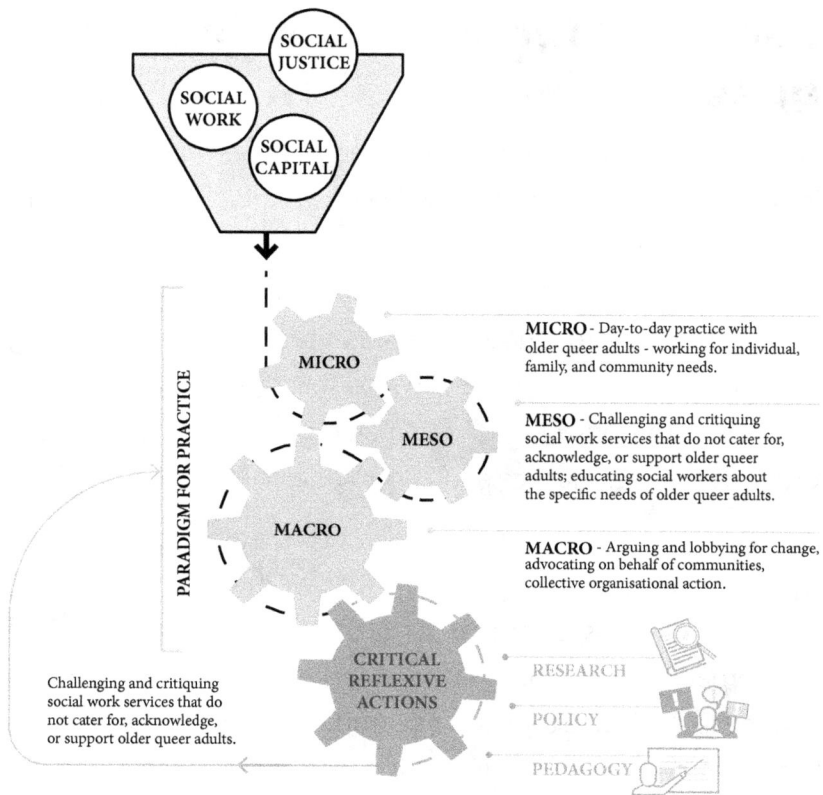

Figure 7.2 Paradigm for practice with older queer adults

and structural levels (Betts, 2023). In this context, social capital can empower practitioners to emphasise the importance of supportive interpersonal relationships, foster community connections, and devise strategies to enhance the exchange of valuable resources. Social work practice at the micro level also entails acknowledging the challenges involved in maintaining or building social capital, whether due to practical constraints, isolation, or internal dynamics within the queer community, and implementing strategies to provide assistance in these situations (Bratt, Stenstrom, and Rennemark, 2017). Operating at this micro level represents the initial step in integrating social justice principles, as it recognises the broader societal shortcomings in catering to the needs of all individuals (O'Brien, 2011).

Meso

The meso level of practice represents the next focal point for social work engagement. Within this realm, the narratives presented in this book highlights the participants' accounts of encountering service providers who failed to recognise their identities, lacked the necessary skills to effectively work with queer adults, and, in some instances, displayed active hostility based on the participants' identity. As social workers, part of our meso level practice involves internally challenging these systems. Social work carries a mandate of social justice, which necessitates ensuring that the profession itself is inclusive and supportive. Therefore, we must critically examine and critique our own profession and institutions when they fall short of meeting these benchmarks (Betts, 2023; O'Brien, 2011).

It is crucial for social work not to become complacent once anti-discrimination legislation is introduced or already in place. We must recognise that diverse and potentially vulnerable communities still require specific services and intervention strategies. Embracing social justice principles in our work with older queer adults at the meso level should incorporate elements of pedagogy to support our ongoing awareness of the evolving needs of all members of society. Social workers must actively engage in educating and teaching their colleagues about the specific needs of older queer adults, integrating research insights and practice reflections to challenge any complacency within social work practices.

Macro

The macro level represents the subsequent stage, encompassing social work practice concerned with broader structural and social transformations. Although this level is often associated with social justice terminology, the principles of social justice underpin the entirety of social work practice. When supporting older queer adults at the macro level, social workers can engage in collective political actions, such as advocacy on behalf of professional social work organisations, lobbying for governmental reforms, and advocating for specific services or interventions (Betts, 2023).

However, operating at the macro level presents challenges for social work. Issues such as funding limitations and collective responsibility arise, as the resources required for extensive collective action may not be readily available to individual social workers. Additionally, the profession of social work may not sufficiently incorporate macro level strategies into its pedagogical practices (Rothman and Mizrahi, 2014). Social workers employed in government services or agencies dependent on centrally funded contracts may hesitate to engage in collective action that could jeopardise their employment or the work of their organisations. Overcoming such challenges is not easy, and there is no one-size-fits-all solution that would enable all practitioners to effectively work at the macro level. However, it remains crucial for social workers and the profession as a whole to remain politically engaged and actively seek opportunities for impactful and critical social action as they arise.

Critical reflexive actions

Ensuring transformative change within social work necessitates action not only in practice but also in research, policy advocacy, and pedagogy. The framework of critical social theory and critical gerontology calls for the integration of critical reflexive actions from practice into other dimensions of social work. As depicted in the practice paradigm (Figure 7.2), the use of critical reflexive actions derived from practice experiences is essential in informing all levels of social work practice.

The first critical reflexive action involves research, specifically the incorporation of discipline-appropriate and up-to-date research to inform social work practice. Practitioners and social services need to integrate recent research findings into their service and practice models in order to stay engaged with contemporary debates, social issues, and the concerns of service users. One approach to support the incorporation of research into practice reflexively is through the involvement of practitioner–researchers. These professionals possess a unique skill set that allows them to draw upon their client work experiences and service knowledge while utilising research skills and techniques to enhance service delivery.

The second reflexive action pertains to policy and advocacy. In addition to incorporating research into frontline practice, social workers should utilise research findings and their practice experiences to inform individual and collective social action targeted at policy change. To effectively address macro social issues, social workers must be informed by research and practice experiences. Furthermore, critical social research and practice will only be effective if social workers embrace the reflexive action of integrating their insights and experiences into advocacy efforts and policy submissions.

The third critical reflexive action focuses on pedagogy. It is crucial to incorporate research findings and practice experiences into social work education. This process should occur in social work training programs, such as tertiary education programs, as well as ongoing professional development undertaken by social workers in Aotearoa New Zealand.

While the practice paradigm depicted in Figure 7.2 is based on the experiences of older queer adults and may not be universally applicable, its application is inherently contextual and should reflect the social worker and the specific social work service. Therefore, the paradigm for practice can be adapted to better address the needs of other population groups, as it remains sensitive to the unique context and requirements of different social work settings.

8

Reshaping social spaces

Reflections on the way forward for social work and older queer adults

Learning objective: to analyse the key content and insights presented in the book regarding older queer adults' engagement with social spaces

By critically reflecting on the material discussed throughout the book, readers will be able to identify and summarise the significant points and understand the implications for older queer adults' wellbeing and sense of community.

Learning objective: to evaluate the potential for advocacy and support for older queer adults based on the findings and discussions in the book

Readers will assess the avenues for further advocacy efforts and explore strategies to provide meaningful support for older queer adults in social work practice. They will also consider the role of educators in utilising the book as a resource to educate emerging students and practitioners in the field of social work, identifying practical ways to integrate the knowledge gained from the book into their educational approaches.

Introduction

> Queerness is not yet here. Queerness is an ideality … Queerness is essentially about the rejection of a here and now and an insistence on potentiality or concrete possibility for another world.
>
> (José Esteban Muñoz, 2019)

Contribution to the wider discussion, the social work profession, and Aotearoa New Zealand

The purpose of this book is to explore how social work can effectively support older queer adults in Aotearoa New Zealand. To achieve this goal, I investigated the connection between social capital and wellbeing while exploring specific aspects such as legislation, social relationships, and practical considerations related to age. I analysed the narratives and stories shared by participants, employing applied thematic analysis to identify common themes and generate meaningful findings. To ensure practical applicability for practitioners, policymakers, and researchers, I developed a conceptual model that outlines the structural factors that impact older queer individuals. Additionally, I created a practice paradigm rooted in social justice, which serves as a framework for implementing the research findings at the micro, meso, and macro levels of intervention.

There and now

A central theme that I have emphasised throughout this book is that the discriminatory experiences faced by older queer individuals are not confined to the past. When writing this research, I frequently encountered a common question: "Why focus on this topic if homosexuality has been legal for decades and marriage equality has been achieved?" I received this question from social work colleagues, members of the public, and even aspiring social work students. This question reflects the prevailing belief that queer individuals no longer encounter discrimination, stigma, or exclusion from mainstream society. There is an assumption that progressive legislation has completely transformed social norms and behaviours. However, the reality has shown that this is not the case. The experiences of discrimination and marginalisation persist, and it is important to address and acknowledge the ongoing challenges faced by older queer individuals. As explored in Chapter 3, the issue at hand is that many of the attitudes that existed prior to legislative reform continue to persist in Aotearoa New Zealand. These attitudes and behaviours manifest in various ways, including direct abuse, discrimination, lack of recognition, and even internal identity politics within the queer community. These examples serve as clear indications of the ongoing presence of these issues in contemporary Aotearoa New Zealand society.

Working within communities: recognising and supporting diverse identities

Through this book, and in the presentation of the narratives of the participants, I have aimed to contribute to the social work profession and the broader discussions surrounding the queer community by challenging the perception of homogeneity within this community. A key aspect of this process has been to emphasise the diverse and intersecting identities among older queer individuals. In Chapter 4, I explored how certain individuals faced fewer obstacles in accessing social spaces based on their sexual and gender identities. On the other hand, in chapters 5 and 6, I examined how age acted as a barrier to social participation. These findings serve as essential considerations for social work practitioners and policymakers, highlighting the need to move away from a one-size-fits-all approach when working with the queer community. Recognising and addressing the unique experiences and challenges faced by individuals with diverse identities is crucial to ensuring inclusivity and avoiding privileging more mainstream identities.

It is however important to readdress one significant limitation of this book – and that is the lack of diversity in the recruitment process regarding race, ethnicity, and culture. While I have aimed to highlight and recognise diverse identities within the queer community, the lack of an intersectional analysis that includes race, ethnicity, and culture is significant. Of particular note is the lack of Māori participants, a factor that is significant considering Aotearoa New Zealand's history as a colonised country, and the implications this has for tangata whenua. At this time I am unable to state definitively why this limitation occurred. It is possible that my recruitment strategies were not sufficiently compressive, or individual factors such as my own ethnicity may have resulted in a lack of Māori participants. This particular limitation has specific considerations for the application of these findings in an Aotearoa New Zealand context. Social work in Aotearoa New Zealand is guided by the Aotearoa Association of Social Workers as well as the Social Workers Registration Board, both of which include competencies about the ability of practitioners to work with Māori communities. These competencies are a result of social work in Aotearoa New Zealand being guided by bicultural principles that recognise the need for supporting Māori interests at all levels of New Zealand society – which includes the provision of social work services. I do hope that the narratives and stories presented within this book prove useful for social workers, however, a critical consideration of their limits, and the experiences they represent, is required by all readers.

Thoughts about language

One reflection that I have been focused on during the writing of this book, and one where there is no easy response, is in regard to the use of language. I discussed the use of language at the beginning of this book, where in Chapter 1 I described my rationale for relying on the terminology of queer. In making that decision, I inevitably created a conflict of intention. The use of queer was intended to reflect the inherent diversity present within the community, critique the fact that the majority of previous research has focused on gay men and lesbian women, and establish at the forefront of this book that the use of queer, or the queering of social structures, is a radical act. Yet the language of heteronormativity and cisnormativity potentially undermine those efforts. It was necessary to establish a framework that explored how social structures based around expectations of sexuality and gender create a system of privilege and disadvantage, and previous research has leaned heavily on the terminology of heteronormativity and cisnormativity to define those relationships (Smith, Shin, and Officer, 2011).

This disjuncture between wanting to acknowledge diversity and the flaws of binary thinking, yet still applying binary language within academic concepts, became more obvious to me throughout the course of writing this book. I do not believe at this stage that I can present a viable alternative, or that such an alternative currently exists. Yet it was important for me to include this reflection because the theoretical framework of this research requires a reflexive critique. What I believe this adds to social work discourses is an increased awareness about the potential use of language in practice, policy, and research – and in particular to acknowledge when there is no easy way to describe social structures or our relationship to them as a community. Language is a powerful force, especially for disadvantaged groups in society (Gendon et al., 2015; Oliver, 2012), and a consideration for how we use terms so easily taken for granted is important for all forms of social work. This consideration reflects the suggestions of the authors Smith, Shin, and Officer (2011, p. 190), who argued that practitioners need to develop "an awareness of the constitutive power of language, the pervasive language that reproduces this binary, and the paradox of socially constructed identity categories." Reflecting on this consideration is important for future studies, but also in the development of practice strategies and policies that are designed to support the queer community.

Reflection

Research is a personal journey. Qualitative research in particular is a reflection of that journey, and the relationship between the research topic, the researcher, and the participants (Kvale, 1996). Throughout the course of working on this book – from developing the initial proposal, contacting and interviewing participants, to analysing the findings – I was constantly learning, reflecting, and journaling what I was experiencing. The topic of this research required me to be critical about my own perspectives, as well as the responsibility I had to present the findings as honestly and sensitively as possible. Part of this process occurred throughout the research interviews, as participants talked about my own identity, noting my age as a comparatively younger adult, and sexual and gender identity as a bisexual cisgender man. As a result, I found myself not only being more aware of how I interpreted the discussions I had with the participants, I found myself also being more aware of these topics in my day-to-day life. My own interpretations and potential assumptions were not the only influencing factor on this research. In one discussion I had with a participant, he talked about his own thoughts and feelings prior to the interview, and who he believed I would be based on my recruitment advertisements and previous correspondence:

> One of the things I tried very hard to do, and I think I succeeded, was not to get any preconceived ideas about yourself and what you were doing and what you were going to ask. So this morning, after breakfast, I just shut off and thought, no I'm going to go into this completely open and blind and awaken. So I didn't want to formulate any questions other than the obvious ones about safety and confidentiality and all that stuff.
>
> (Liam, 68)

The advertisements that I distributed for this research had minimal information about myself. It described this research project, its goals, as well as mentioning that this was a social work-driven project. Some recruitment advertisements were edited by distributors to include my sexual orientation, but aside from those alterations, the advertisements were consistent. If there had been different information about my own background and identity it is possible to assume that the sample pool of the participants in this research might have been different.

Influence on practice

During the course of working on this research, I was also practicing as a social worker. An unexpected outcome of these dual roles was that I felt my own ability to engage, practice, and work with clients was enhanced by the interviews I conducted with the participants in this research. The participants I talked with were all honest, open, and provided a complex set of lived experiences and insights. As James disclosed to me:

> As I say, I've been totally open with you, because I've got nothing to lose now, I'm at that time of life when these things are no longer such a major issue, because I'm in the twilight years if you like.
>
> (James, 70)

While another participant touched upon the multitude of stories they had, and the inherent reflexivity the interview process provided:

> There's millions of stories, David. It's really interesting doing this process, for me, because it stimulates my memory. And I'm thinking, oh there's so much in there, yeah, of life stories about that time.
>
> (Hannah, 72)

Being in the role of a researcher and actively engaging with the participants of this book has provided me with invaluable insights on how to effectively collaborate with clients from diverse backgrounds. Surprisingly, I discovered that the openness and willingness of the participants to share their experiences went beyond the mere fulfilment of research objectives. It highlighted the remarkable opportunities that social work research presents to researchers. These opportunities extend beyond the scope of simply answering research questions.

In fact, during my fourth interview, the impact of this experience struck me so profoundly that I felt compelled to reflect on it in a journal entry. I realised that the process of connecting with participants on a personal level allowed me to better understand their unique perspectives, challenges, and strengths. It fostered a deeper sense of empathy and compassion within me, reinforcing the notion that social work research is not solely about gathering data, but also about building meaningful connections and promoting positive change.

Engaging with participants in this study has not only enriched my research journey but has also enhanced my ability to work alongside individuals from diverse backgrounds in my future social work practice. It has underscored the significance of creating a safe and trusting environment for clients to share their stories, allowing us to develop more effective interventions and support systems tailored to their specific needs. Through this experience, I have come to appreciate the transformative power of genuine human connection in social work research and practice, transcending the boundaries of academia and positively impacting the lives of those we serve.

This research and the writing of this book has as much been a personal journey for me as it has been about exploring the social networks and wellbeing of older queer adults. While every effort has been made to present a transparent description of the research, analysis process, and presentation of the findings, this book is influenced by my own experiences over the last decade. The personal and reflexive nature of this type of research is not a limitation; rather, it is just an acknowledgement of the nuanced dynamics that are always present within qualitative social research and inherent to all forms of social work practice.

Concluding thoughts

The task of supporting all older queer individuals undoubtedly requires substantial future work. It is crucial to acknowledge their ongoing experiences of discrimination and stigma, the concerns surrounding professional competency and services, and the internal dynamics within the queer community that may inadvertently exclude certain identities. However, one critical aspect that demands particular attention from social workers is how older queer adults engage with social spaces.

Throughout this book, my primary goal has been to shed light on the experiences of older queer individuals, amplify their voices, and advocate for a more critical and inclusive approach within the social work profession. In doing so, it has become evident that understanding how older queer adults navigate social spaces is a key component of providing effective support. Whether it's accessing community centres, joining social groups, or participating in events, social spaces play a significant role in the lives of older queer individuals. These spaces offer opportunities for connection, belonging, and the formation of support networks. However, they can also present challenges and barriers that need to be addressed.

By giving voice to the experiences shared by older queer adults, we can better comprehend their engagement with social spaces. Some may describe the ease with which they access these spaces is based on their sexual and gender identities. However, for others, age can become a barrier, limiting their social participation and sense of inclusion.

To adequately support older queer adults in their engagement with social spaces, it is imperative that social workers, organisations, professional bodies, and researchers come together. We must critically examine the existing structures and dynamics of these spaces, and identify and address any systemic biases or exclusionary practices that hinder the full participation of older queer individuals. This collective effort requires a comprehensive approach, involving frontline practitioners who interact directly with older queer adults, the organisations that provide support services, professional bodies that guide and support practitioners, and ongoing research that informs the development of inclusive strategies for practice.

By actively involving older queer adults in shaping social spaces, fostering a sense of ownership and agency, and addressing the barriers they face, we can create social environments that are truly inclusive and affirming. It is through this collaborative and intentional effort that we can ensure older queer adults feel welcomed, valued, and fully engaged in the social spaces that are vital for their wellbeing and overall quality of life. As Liam reflected on at the end of our interview together:

One of the things that our conversation has brought more and more home to me, is that how big this issue is actually. It's a very important one. I think mental health, or health, or wellbeing in general for this increasingly ageing group of people, is huge in this country. And we need to support each other.

(Liam, 68)

Recommended assignments and activities

1 Assignment prompt: analyse the impact of social policy and legislation on older queer adults

This prompt is appropriate for subjects related to social work, social science, or humanities, which involve the evaluation of social policies and/or legislation. The focus of the assignment need not be exclusively on the requirements or encounters of older queer adults. Instead, it can be employed as an instance to investigate how modifications in social policies and legislation impact specific communities. Educators must modify the assignment to match the legislative framework of their specific region, and the professional discipline in which they teach.

Learning objectives:

- To analyse the impact of changes in social policy and legislation on the experiences of older queer adults.

- To demonstrate critical thinking skills by analysing a piece of legislation or social policy that affects the queer community.
- To formulate an innovative policy change that will positively impact the queer community using knowledge and insight.
- To reflect on the importance of legislation and social change in social work or related discipline.

Instructions:

Part 1: Analysis of a piece of legislation or social policy

1. Choose a piece of legislation or social policy that impacts the queer community.
2. Read and summarise the key provisions of the legislation or policy.
3. Evaluate the effectiveness of the legislation or policy in addressing the needs of older queer adults.
4. Identify any gaps or limitations in the legislation or policy that negatively impact the queer community.

Part 2: Innovative policy change

1. Based on your analysis, develop an innovative policy change that addresses the gaps and limitations identified in the legislation or policy.
2. Outline the key provisions of your innovative policy change, including its objectives, target population, and funding mechanisms (if applicable).
3. Evaluate the potential impact of your innovative policy change on the lives of older queer adults.
4. Provide evidence and reasoning to support the effectiveness of your proposed policy change.

Part 3: Reflection on the relationship between legislation and social change

1. Reflect on the importance of understanding the relationship between legislation and social change in social work (or related discipline).
2. Discuss how social work (or professional) values, roles, and skills can influence and support the development and implementation of innovative policy change.
3. Analyse the potential impact of your innovative policy change on the broader social work practice and the advancement of social justice.

2 Reflective activity prompt: considering assumptions about the queer community

This reflective activity prompt is suited for courses and subjects linked to social work, social sciences, and humanities. It is also beneficial for professionals actively working in social work and human services roles. Educators can customise this prompt to cater to their classroom audience and their ability to engage in suitable critical reflection. Professional supervisors and practitioners are urged to utilise these prompts in their supervisory role, either individually or in a group setting, and modify them as necessary to align with their present work setting.

Prompt:

After reading the Chapter 1 on how different members of the queer community are able to access and engage with queer spaces based on their sexual and gender identities, take a moment to reflect on your assumptions about the queer community. Consider the following questions:

1. Did you assume that all members of the queer community have the same experiences and face the same challenges when accessing queer spaces? If so, why do you think you made this assumption?

2. Were there any new insights or information presented in the chapter that challenged your assumptions about the queer community?

3. What is the value in engaging with and supporting the queer community, particularly for those who may not feel included as part of that community?

4. In what ways can you advocate for the queer community, even if you do not identify as part of that community yourself?

5. How might your own experiences and identity influence your approach to engaging with and supporting the queer community?

Take some time to reflect on these questions and consider how your perspective on the queer community may have shifted as a result of reading this chapter.

Consider how you can use this new understanding to be a more effective ally and advocate for the queer community.

3 Learning activity prompt: designing inclusive social spaces – a practical exercise

This activity is designed to engage students and practitioners in designing inclusive social spaces that support the needs and wellbeing of older queer adults at micro, meso, and macro levels of social work practice. This learning activity would be suitable for undergraduate courses in social work, gerontology, queer studies, or courses that focus on diversity and inclusion.

Instructions:

1. Divide participants into small groups (3–4 members per group).

2. Provide each group with a scenario depicting a social space (e.g., healthcare facility, community centre, residential care home) where older queer adults seek support and engagement.

3. Instruct each group to brainstorm and discuss strategies and interventions that social workers can implement at micro, meso, and macro levels to create an inclusive and supportive environment for older queer adults in the given scenario.

4. Encourage participants to draw on the content of this book including the conceptual model and paradigm for practice, to inform their discussions.

5. Give each group 15–20 minutes to develop a list of recommendations and interventions that address the unique challenges faced by older queer adults in their designated social space.

6. After the allotted time, reconvene as a whole group and have each group present their recommendations and interventions. Allow for open discussion and feedback.

7. Facilitate a reflective debrief by asking questions such as:

    a. What were some common themes or strategies identified across the groups?

    b. How do the recommendations align with the principles of social justice and the structural forces impacting older queer adults discussed in the book?

    c. What are the potential barriers or challenges in implementing these strategies, and how can they be overcome?

    d. How can social workers collaborate with other professionals and stakeholders to advocate for change and create more inclusive social spaces?

8. Conclude the activity by summarising the key takeaways and reinforcing the importance of designing inclusive social spaces to support the wellbeing of older queer adults.

This learning activity encourages students and practitioners to actively engage with the chapter content, apply theoretical knowledge to real-life scenarios, and collaboratively develop practical strategies for social work practice. It promotes critical thinking, problem-solving, and creative approaches to address the unique challenges faced by older queer adults within social spaces.

Notes

1. Throughout this book quotes by older queer adults are used, all of whom I interviewed to hear their experiences, stories, and insights. Each participant has been given a first-name pseudonym to protect their identity and privacy, and the number next to each pseudonym indicates the age of the participant at the time of the interview.

2. Pākehā is the Māori word for New Zealanders of European descent.

3. Judith Collins is a National Party MP, who at the time was opposed to the Civil Union Act (2004).

4. Described as a movement from the late 1960s to the mid-1980s that focused on advancing the rights of the queer community.

5. Sisters for Homophile Equality was the first national lesbian organisation in New Zealand, established in Christchurch in 1973.

6. Scene spaces are defined as a range of city venues, such as cafes, pubs, and clubs, frequented and recognised by the queer community as safe, accessible, and commercially available.

7. The Dorian Society existed between 1962 and 1988, and was New Zealand's first organisation for homosexual men.

8. While the participant in this interview used the term "transsexual" to refer to themselves, the term is considered as potentially offensive and outdated as of today, with many members of the queer community preferring to use the term transgender instead. The term "transsexual," however, is still used by many older adults, who grew up hearing and identifying with this language. The quote in question

has been presented without alteration, however critical consideration of its use should be considered by readers.

9. The name of the organisation was removed to protect the confidentiality of the interviewee and the organisation.

10. The name of the organisation was removed to protect the confidentiality of the interviewee and the organisation.

11. The name of the healthcare service was anonymised to protect confidentiality.

12. The name of the retirement village was anonymised to protect confidentiality.

References

Abendstern, M., Harrington, V., Brand, C., Tucker, S., Wilberforce, M., and Challis, D. (2012). Variations in structures, processes and outcomes of community mental health teams for older people: A systematic review of the literature. *Aging and Mental Health*, 16(7), pp. 861–873. https://doi.org/10.1080/13607863.2011.651431

Antonelli, P. and Dettore, D. (2014). Relationship, social, and individual wellbeing in Italian male same-sex couples. *Journal of Gay and Lesbian Social Services*, 26(3), pp. 383–406. https://doi.org/10.1080/10538720.2014.926231

ANZASW. (2015). *Code of Ethics*. Available at: https://anzasw.nz/summary-of-the-code-of-ethics/#1455661580585-cc40fe31-8b3a

Barker, J. and Thomson, L. (2015). Helpful relationships with service users: Linking social capital. *Australian Social Work*, 68(1), pp. 130–145. https://doi.org/10.1080/0312407X.2014.905795

Baum, F. E. and Ziersch, A. M. (2003). Social capital. *Journal of Epidemiology and Community Health*, 57(5), pp. 320–323. https://doi.org/10.1136/jech.57.5.320

Behrmann, J. and Ravitsky, V. (2013). Queer liberation, not elimination: Why selecting against intersex is not "straight" forward. *The American Journal of Bioethics*, 13(10), pp. 39–41. https://doi.org/10.1080/15265161.2013.828131

Bergh, N. V. D. and Crisp, C. (2004). Defining culturally competent practice with sexual minorities: Implications for social work education and practice. *Journal of Social Work Education*, 40(2), pp. 221–238. https://doi.org/10.1080/10437797.2004.10778491

Betts, D. (2023). Social work with older LGBTQ+ adults. In: J. Maidment, R. Egan, R. Tudor, and S. Nipperess (eds.), *Practice Skills for Social Work and Welfare: More Than Just Common Sense.* 4th ed. New York and London: Routledge. https://doi.org/10.4324/9781003198598

Blair, J. P. and Carroll, M. C. (2008). Social capital. *Economic Development Journal,* 7(3), pp. 42–49.

Bratt, A. S., Stenstrom, U., and Rennemark, M. (2017). Effects on life satisfaction of older adults after child and spouse bereavement. *Aging and Mental Health,* 21(6), pp. 602–608. https://doi.org/10.1080/13607863.2015.1135874

Brennan-Ing, M., Seidel, L., Larson, B., and Karprak, S. E. (2014). Social care networks and older LGBT adults: Challenges for the future. *Journal of Homosexuality,* 61(1), pp. 21–52. https://doi.org/10.1080/00918369.2013.835235

Brickell, C. (2008). *Mates and Lovers: A History of Gay New Zealand.* Auckland: Godwit, Random House New Zealand.

Brooke, L. and Taylor, P. (2005). Older workers and employment: Managing age relations. *Ageing and Society,* 25(3), pp. 415–429. https://doi.org/10.1017/S0144686X05003466

Brown, K. (2006). *Vulnerable Adults and Community Care.* UK: Learning Matter.

Carpenter, M. (2016). The human rights of intersex people: Addressing harmful practices and rhetoric of change. *Reproductive Health Matters,* 24(47), pp. 74–84. https://doi.org/10.1016/j.rhm.2016.06.003

Casey, M. (2007). The queer unwanted and their undesirable otherness. In: J. Lim and K. Bowne (eds.), *Geographies of Sexualities: Theory, Practices and Politics.* Aldershot: Ashgate.

Chambers, P. (2004). The case for critical social gerontology in social work education and older women. *Social Work Education:*

The International Journal, 23(6), pp. 745–758. https://doi.org/10.1080/0261547042000294518

Chandler, M., Margery, M., Maynard, N., Newsome, M., South, C., Panich, E. and Payne, R. (2004). Sexuality, older people and residential aged care. *Geriaction,* 22(4), pp. 5–11.

Choi, N. G. and Kim, J. (2011). The effect of time volunteering and charitable donations in later life on psychological wellbeing. *Aging and Society,* 31(4), pp. 590–610. https://doi.org/10.1017/S0144686X10001224

Civil Unions Act 2004 (NZ). https://www.legislation.govt.nz/act/public/2004/0102/latest/whole.html

Craig, G. (2002). Poverty, social work and social justice. *British Journal of Social Work,* 32(2), pp. 669–682. https://doi.org/10.1093/bjsw/32.6.669

Croghan, C. F., Moone, R. P., and Olson, A. M. (2014). Friends, family, and caregiving among midlife and older lesbian, gay, bisexual and transgender adults. *Journal of Homosexuality,* 61(1), pp. 79–102. https://doi.org/10.1080/00918369.2013.835238

Cronin, A. and King, A. (2010). Power, inequality and identification: Exploring diversity and intersectionality amongst older LGB adults. *Sociology,* 44(5), pp. 876–892. https://doi.org/10.1177/0038038510375738

Dant, T. (2003). *Critical Social Theory: Culture, Society and Critique.* London: Sage Publications.

Davey, J. A. and Cornwall, J. (2007). *Maximising the Potential of Older Workers.* Wellington : New Zealand Institute for Research on Ageing, Victoria University of Wellington.

Duffy, F. and Healy, J. P. (2011). Social work with older people in a hospital setting. *Social Work in Health Care,* 50(2), pp. 109–123. https://doi.org/10.1080/00981389.2010.527786

Erickson-Schroth, L. and Mitchell, J. (2009). Queering queer theory, or why bisexuality matters. *Journal of Bisexuality*, 9(3–4), pp. 297–315. https://doi.org/10.1080/15299710903316596

Ewikj, H. V. (2009). Citizenship-based social work. *International Social Work*, 52(2), pp. 167–179. https://doi.org/10.1177/00208 72808099728

Fenaughty, J. and Pega, F. (2016). Why marriage equality is not enough: Enduring social policy concerns for gender- and sexually diverse New Zealanders. In: L. Beddoe and J. Maidment (eds.), *Social Policy for Social Work and Human Services in Aotearoa New Zealand: Diverse Perspectives*, pp. 223–236. Christchurch: Canterbury University Press.

Fine, B. (2007). Social capital. *Development in Practice*, 17(4–5), pp. 566–574.

Fook, J. (2002). *Social Work: Critical Theory and Practice*. London: Sage Publications.

Forrest, R. and Kearns, A. (2001). Social cohesion, social capital and the neighbourhood. *Urban Studies*, 38(12), pp. 2125–2143. https://doi.org/10.1080/00420980120087081

Fox, R. C. (2007). Gay grows up: An interpretive study on aging metaphors and queer identity. *Journal of Homosexuality*, 52(3–4), pp. 33–61. https://doi.org/10.1300/J082v52n03_03

Fredriksen-Goldsen, K. I. and Muraco, A. (2010). Aging and sexual orientation: A 25-year review of the literature. *Research on Aging*, 32(3), pp. 372–413. https://doi.org/10.1177/0164027509360355

Fredriksen-Goldsen, K. I., Cook-Daniels, L., Kim, H.-J., Erosheva, E. A., Emlet, C. A., Hoy-Ellis, C. P., Goldsen, J., and Muraco, A. (2014). Physical and mental health of transgender older adults: An at-risk and underserved population. *The Gerontologist*, 54(3), pp. 488–500. https://doi.org/10.1093/geront/gnt021

Fredriksen-Goldsen, K. I., Kim, H., Barkan, S. E., Muraco, A., and Hoy-Ellis, C. P. (2013). Health disparities among lesbian, gay, and bisexual older adults: Results from a population-based study. *American Journal of Public Health*, 103(10), pp. 1802–1809. https://doi.org/10.2105/AJPH.2012.301110

Fredriksen-Goldsen, K. I., Kim, H., Emlet, C. A., Muraco, A., Erosheva, E. A., Hoy-Ellis, C. P., Goldsen, J., and Petry, H. (2011). *The aging and health report: Disparities and resilience among lesbian, gay, bisexual, and transgender older adults*. Available at: http://caringandaging.org/wordpress/wp-content/uploads/2011/05/Full-Report-FINAL-11-16-11.pdf

Fredriksen-Goldsen, K. I., Kim, H., Shiu, C., Goldsen, J., and Emlet, C. A. (2015). Successful aging among LGBT older adults: Physical and mental health-related quality of life by age group. *The Gerontologist*, 55(1), 154–168. https://doi.org/10.1093/geront/gnu081

Freeman, M. and Vasconcelos, E. F. S. (2010). Critical social theory: Core tenants, inherent issues. *Critical Social Theory Evaluation Practice*, 127, pp. 7–19.

Freixas, A., Luque, B., and Reina, A. (2012). Critical feminist gerontology: In the back rooms of research. *Journal of Women and Aging*, 24(1), pp. 44–58. https://doi.org/10.1080/08952841.2012.638891

Fronek, P. (2012). *Issues in Ageing for Lesbian, Gay, Bisexual, Transgender and Intersex (LGBTI) People*. Available at: www.podsocs.com/podcast/issues-in-ageing-for-lesbian-gay-bisexual-transgender-and-intersex-people/

Fuss, D. (1991). Inside/out. In: D. Fuss (ed.), *Inside/Out: Lesbian Theories, Gay Theories* (pp. 1–10). New York and London: Routledge.

Gendon, T. L., Welleford, E. A., Inker, J., and White, J. T. (2015). The language of ageism: Why we need to use words carefully. *The Gerontologist*, 55(6), pp. 997–1006. https://doi.org/10.1093/geront/gnv066

Gorman-Murray, A., Sullivan, C., and Baganz, E. (2022). Ageing, sexualities and place: Aligning the geographies of gerontology and sexualities. *Geography Compass*, 16(8). https://doi.org/10.1111/gec3.12655

Green, A, I. (2007). Queer theory and sociology: Locating the subject and the self in sexuality studies. *Sociological Theory*, 25(1), pp. 26–45. https://doi.org/10.1111/j.1467-9558.2007.00296.x

Guess, R. (1981). *The Idea of a Critical Theory: Habermas and the Frankfurt School*. London: Cambridge University Press.

Healy, K. and Hampshire, A. (2002). Social capital: A useful concept for social work? *Australian Social Work*, 55(3), pp. 227–238. https://doi.org/10.1080/03124070208410978

Henrickson, M., Neville, S., Jordan, C., and Donaghey, S. (2007). Lavender Islands: The New Zealand study. *Journal of Homosexuality*, 43(4), pp. 223–248. https://doi.org/10.1080/00918360802103514

Homosexual Law Reform Act 1986 (NZ). https://www.legislation.govt.nz/act/public/1986/0033/latest/whole.html

Hicklin, A. (2016). David Bowie: An obituary. *Out*. [Online]. Available at: https://www.out.com/music/2016/1/11/david-bowie-obituary

Hughes, A. K., Harold, R. D., and Boyer, J. M. (2011). Awareness of LGBT aging issues among aging services network providers. *Journal of Gerontological Social Work*, 54(7), pp. 659–677.

Hughes, M. (2010). Expectations of later life support among lesbian and gay Queenslanders. *Australian Journal on Ageing*, 29(4), pp. 161–166. https://doi.org/10.1111/j.1741-6612.2010.00427.x

Hughes, M. and Heycox, K. (2010). *Older People, Ageing and Social Work: Knowledge for Practice*. Sydney: Allen and Unwin.

Hughes, M. and Kentlyn, S. (2011). Older LGBT people's care networks and communities of practice: A brief note. *International Social Work*, 54(3), pp. 436–444. https://doi.org/10.1177/0020872810396254

Human Rights Act 1993 (NZ). https://www.legislation.govt.nz/act/public/1993/0082/latest/DLM304212.html

International Federation of Social Workers. (2023). *Global Definition of Social Work*. Available at: http://ifsw.org/policies/definition-of-social-work/.

Intersexion. (2012). [DVD] New Zealand: Keir, J. (producer) and Lahood, G. (director), Ponsonby Productions Limited.

Johnson, M. J., Jackson, N. C., Arnete, J. K., and Koffman, S. D. (2005). Gay and lesbian perceptions of discrimination in retirement care facilities. *Journal of Homosexuality*, 49(2), pp. 83–102. https://doi.org/10.1300/J082v49n02_05

Kane, M. N. (2004). Ageism and intervention: What social work students believe about treating people differently because of age. *Educational Gerontology*, 30(9), pp. 767–784. https://doi.org/10.1080/03601270490498098

Keenan, E. K., Limone, C., and Sandoval S. L. (2016). A "just sense of wellbeing": Social work's unifying purpose in action. *Social Work*, 62(1), pp. 19–28. https://doi.org/10.1093/sw/sww066

Kim, K., Lehning, A. J., and Sacco, P. (2016). Assessing the factor structure of wellbeing in older adults: Findings from the national health and aging trends study. *Aging and Mental Health*, 20(8), pp. 814–822. https://doi.org/10.1080/13607863.2015.1037245

Kvale, S. (1996). *InterViews: An Introduction to Qualitative Research Interviewing*. London: Sage Publications.

Laurie, A. (2011a). *Early Groups*. Available at: www.pridenz.com/queer_history_early_groups.html

Laurie, A. (2011b). *Gay Liberation*. Available at: www.pridenz.com/queer_history_gay_liberation.html

Laurie, A. (2011c). *Meeting Places*. Available at: www.pridenz.com/queer_history_meeting_places.html

Lemish, D. and Muhlbauer, V. (2012). "Can't have it all": Representations of older women in popular culture. *Women and Therapy*, 35(3–4), pp. 165–180. https://doi.org/10.1080/02703149.2012.684541

Levitt, H. M. and Ippolito, M. R. (2014). Being transgender: Navigating minority stressors and developing authentic self-presentation. *Psychology of Women Quarterly*, 38(1), pp. 46–64. https://doi.org/10.1177/0361684313501644

Logie, C., Bridge, T. J. and Bridge, P. D. (2007). Evaluating the phobias, attitudes, and cultural competence of Master of Social Work students toward the LGBT populations. *Journal of Homosexuality*, 53(4), pp. 201–221. https://doi.org/10.1080/00918360802103472

Marriage (Definition of Marriage) Amendment Act 2013 (NZ). https://www.legislation.govt.nz/act/public/2013/0020/latest/DLM4505003.html

MacKinnon, S. T. (2009). Social work intellectuals in the twenty-first century: Critical social theory, critical social work and public engagement. *Social Work Education: The International Journal*, 28(5), pp. 512–527. https://doi.org/10.1080/02615470802406494

McLean, K. (2008). Inside, outside, nowhere: Bisexual men and women in the gay and lesbian community. *Journal of Bisexuality*, 8(1–2), pp. 63–80. https://doi.org/10.1080/15299710802143174

Mental Health Commission. (2009). *Mental Health and Social Inclusion: Concepts and Measurements*. Wellington, NZ: Mental Health Commission X. https://ndhadeliver.natlib.govt.nz/delivery/DeliveryManagerServlet?dps_pid=IE1711144

Meyer, D. (2008). Interpreting and expiring anti-queer violence: Race, class, and gender differences among LGBT hate crime victims. *Race, Gender and Class*, 15(3–4), pp. 262–282.

Meyer, I. H. (2003). Prejudice, social stress, and mental health in lesbian, gay, and bisexual populations: Conceptual issues and research evidence. *Psychological Bulletin*, 129(5), pp. 674–697. https://doi.org/10.1037/0033-2909.129.5.674

Mohan, G. and Mohan, J. (2002). Placing social capital. *Progress in Human Geography*, 26(2), pp. 191–210. https://doi.org/10.1191/0309132502ph364ra

Moir, J. (2015). Sex change surgery policy "nutty". *Stuff.* [Online]. Available at: www.stuff.co.nz/national/politics/68670002/sex-change-surgery-policy-nutty

Moir, J. (2016). Homosexual Law Reform 30 years on—what was life like for the gay community pre-1986? *Stuff,* [Online]. Available at: https://i.stuff.co.nz/national/politics/81894181/hom osexual-law-reform-30-years-on--what-was-life-like-for-the-gay-community-pre1986

Morley, C., Macfarlane, S., and Ablett, P. (2014). *Engaging with Social Work: A Critical Introduction.* Port Melbourne, Victoria: Cambridge University Press.

Muñoz, J. (2019). *Cruising Utopia, 10th Anniversary Edition: The Then and There of Queer Futurity.* New York, USA: New York University Press.

Narushima, M. (2005). "Payback time": Community volunteering among older adults as a transformative mechanism. *Aging and Society*, 25(4), pp. 567–584. https://doi.org/10.1017/S0144686X0 5003661

Neville, S. and Henrickson, M. (2010). "Lavender retirement": A questionnaire survey of lesbian, gay and bisexual people's accommodation plans for old age. *International Journal of Nursing Practice*, 16(10), pp. 586–594. https://doi.org/10.1111/j.1440-172X.2010.01885.x

Nyqvist, F., Cattan, M., Andersson, L., Forsman, A. K., and Gustafson, Y. (2013). Social capital and loneliness among the very old living at home and in institutional settings: A comparative study. *Journal of Aging and Health*, 25(6), pp. 1013–1035. https://doi.org/10.1177/0898264313497508

O'Brien, M. (2011). Social justice: Alive and well (partly) in social work practice? *International Social Work*, 54(20), pp. 174–190. https://doi.org/10.1177/0020872810382682

Oliver, C. (2012). Critical realist grounded theory: A new approach for social work research. *British Journal of Social Work*, 42(2), pp. 371–387. https://doi.org/10.1093/bjsw/bcr064

Oxoby, R. (2009). Understanding social inclusion, social cohesion, and social capital. *International Journal of Social Economics*, 36(12), pp. 1133–1152. https://doi.org/10.1108/03068290910996963

Parker, R., Garcia, J., and Munoz-Laboy, M. (2014). Sexual social movements and communities. In: D. L. Tolman and L. M. Diamond (eds.), *APA Handbook of Sexuality and Psycholog: Vol. 2. Contextual Approaches*, pp. 229–250. Washington, DC: American Psychological Association.

Pawar, M. (2006). "Social" "capital"? *The Social Science Journal*, 43(2), pp. 211–226.

Richardson, D. (2017). Rethinking sexual citizenship. *Sociology*, 51(2), pp. 208–224. https://doi.org/10.1177/0038038515609024

Robinson, J. L. and Rubin, L. J. (2016). Homonegative microaggressions and posttraumatic stress symptoms. *Journal of Gay and Lesbian Mental Health*, 20(1), pp. 57–69. https://doi.org/10.1080/19359705.2015.1066729

Rothman, J. and Mizrahi, T. (2014). Balancing micro and macro practice: a challenge for social work. *Social Work*, 59(1), pp. 91–93. https://doi.org/10.1093/sw/swt067

Rowntree, M. R. (2014). Making sexuality visible in Australian social work education. *Social Work Education: The International Journal*, 33(3), pp. 353–364. https://doi.org/10.1080/02615479.2013.834885

Seligman, M. E. P. (2011). *Flourish: A Visionary New Understanding of Happiness and Wellbeing*. New York: Free Press.

Settersten, R. A., Jr. and Hagestad, G. O. (2015). Subjective ageing and new complexities of the life course. *Annual Review of Gerontology and Geriatrics*, 35(1), pp. 29–53. https://doi.org/10.1891/0198-8794.35.29

Sharek, D. B., McCann, E., Sheerin, F., Glacken, M., and Higgins, A. (2015). Older LGBT people's experiences and concerns with healthcare professionals and services in Ireland. *International Journal of Older People Nursing*, 10(3), pp. 230–240. https://doi.org/10.1111/opn.12078

Shenman, G. and Shmotkin, D. (2016). The hostile-world scenario and mental health concomitants among gays and lesbians. *Journal of Gay and Lesbian Mental Health,* 20(1), pp. 70–86. https://doi.org/10.1080/19359705.2015.1048915

Shortt, S. E. D. (2004). Making sense of social capital, health and policy. *Health Policy*, 70(1), pp. 11–22. https://doi.org/10.1016/j.healthpol.2004.01.007

Siverskog, A. (2014). "They just don't have a clue": Transgender aging and implications for social work. *Journal of Gerontological Social Work*, 57(2–4), pp. 386–406. https://doi.org/10.1080/01634372.2014.895472

Smith, L. C., Shin, R. Q., and Officer, L. M. (2011). Moving counselling forward on LGB and transgender issues: Speaking queerly on discourses and microaggressions. *The Counselling Psychologist*, 40(3), pp. 385–408. https://doi.org/10.1177/0011000011403165

Statistics New Zealand. (2013). *People Aged 65+ Living in New Zealand*. Available at: www.stats.govt.nz/infographics/people-aged-65-plus-living-in-new-zealand

Stuff. (2009, July 24). *The Real Helen Clark*. [Online] Available at: www.stuff.co.nz/national/politics/2607353/The-real-Helen-Clark

Stuff. (2012, November 5). *Key Criticises Show Host Over "Gay Red Top."* [Online] Available at: www.stuff.co.nz/national/politics/7908160/Key-criticises-show-host-over-gay-red-top

Sullivan, N. (2003). *A Critical Introduction to Queer Theory*. Edinburgh University Press. https://doi.org/10.1515/9781474472944

SuperSeniors. (2016). *Our Ageing Population*. Available at: www.superseniors.msd.govt.nz/about-superseniors/media/key-statistics.html

SWRB. (2023). *Social Workers Registration Board: Code of Conduct*. Retrieved from: https://swrb.govt.nz/practice/code-of-conduct

Talo, C., Mannarini, T., and Rochira, A. (2014). Sense of community and community participation: A meta-analytic review. *Social Indicators Research*, 117(1), pp. 1–28. https://doi.org/10.1007/s11205-013-0347-2

Taylor, Y. (2007). "If your face doesn't fit…": The misrecognition of working-class lesbians in scene space. *Leisure Studies,* 26(2), pp. 161–178. https://doi.org/10.1080/02614360600661211

Taylor, Y. (2008). "That's not really my scene": Working-class lesbians in (and out of) place. *Sexualities*, 11(5), pp. 523–546. https://doi.org/10.1177/1363460708094266

Templeton Prize. (2013). Who we are: Human uniqueness and the African spirit of Ubuntu. Desmond Tutu, Templeton Prize 2013. Available at: www.youtube.com/watch?v=0wZtfqZ271w

Theurer, K. and Wister, A. (2010). Altruistic behaviour and social capital as predictors of wellbeing among older Canadians. *Aging and Society*, 30(1), pp. 157–181. https://doi.org/10.1017/S0144686X09008848

Torche, F. and Valenzuela, E. (2011). Trust and reciprocity: A theoretical distinction of the sources of social capital. *European Journal of Social Theory*, 14(2), pp. 181–198. https://doi.org/10.1177/1368431011403461

Le Guin, U. K. "American SF and the Other" in *Science-Fiction Studies* 7, 1975. Reprinted in The Language of the Night, 1979.

Van Wagenen, A., Driskell, J., and Bradford, J. (2013). "I'm still raring to go": Successful aging among lesbian, gay, bisexual, and transgender older adults. *Journal of Aging Studies*, 27(1), pp. 1–14. https://doi.org/10.1016/j.jaging.2012.09.001

Veldorale-Griffin, A. (2014). Transgender science: How might it shape the way we think about transgender rights? *Journal of GLBT Family Studies*, 10(5), pp. 475–501.

Volpp, S. Y. (2010). What about the "B" in LGB: Are bisexual women's mental health issues same or different? *Journal of Gay and Lesbian Mental Health*, 14(1), pp. 41–51. https://doi.org/10.1080/193597 00903416016

Weeks, J. (1998). The sexual citizen. *Theory, Culture and Society*, 15(3–4), pp. 35–52. https://doi.org/10.1177/026327649801 5003003

Willett, G. and Brickell, C. (2016). LGBTIQ activism in Australia and New Zealand. In: *Encyclopaedia of Gender and Sexuality Studies*, Malden, MA: Wiley-Blackwell, pp. 1–5.

Willis, P., Maegusuku-Hewett, T., Raithby, M., and Miles, P. (2016). Swimming upstream: The provision of inclusive care to older lesbian, gay and bisexual (LGB) adults in residential and nursing environments in Wales. *Ageing and Society*, 36(2), pp. 282–306. https://doi.org/10.1017/S0144686X14001147

Wilson, L. (2006). Developing a model for the measurement of social inclusion and social capital in regional Australia. *Social Indicators Research*, 75(3), pp. 335–360. https://doi.org/10.1007/ s11205-004-2527-6

Wilson, S. (2017, May 16). What else did Alfred Ngaro say on that "naïve" weekend? [Online] The Spinoff. Available at: https://the spinoff.co.nz/politics/16-05-2017/what-else-did-alfred-ngaro-say-on-that-naive-weekend

Yeung, P., Good, G., O'Donoghue, K., Spence, S., and Ros, B. (2017). What matters most to people in retirement villages and their transition to residential aged care. *Aotearoa New Zealand Social Work*, 29(4), pp. 84–96. https://doi.org/10.11157/anzswj-vol29is s4id419

Recommended further reading

Hunter, S. (2005). *Midlife and older LGBT adults: Knowledge and affirmative practice for the social services*. New York and London: Routledge.

Lim, J. and Browne, K. (2007). *Geographies of sexualities: Theory, practices and politics*. New York and London: Routledge.

Naylor, L. A. (2021). *Social equity and LGBTQ rights: Dismantling discrimination and expanding civil rights*. New York and London: Routledge.

Index